Angelina Virginia Walton Winkler

# Souvenir of the Twin Cities of North Carolina

Angelina Virginia Walton Winkler

**Souvenir of the Twin Cities of North Carolina**

ISBN/EAN: 9783337253974

Printed in Europe, USA, Canada, Australia, Japan

Cover: Foto ©Thomas Meinert / pixelio.de

More available books at **www.hansebooks.com**

Salem Female Academy.—Main and South Halls.

# SOUVENIR

OF THE

TWIN CITIES OF NORTH CAROLINA,

# WINSTON--SALEM,

FORSYTH COUNTY.

## DESCRIPTIVE AND HISTORICAL

*BY MRS. A. V. WINKLER.*

"Facts, sir! facts are stubborn things."—DICKENS.

SALEM, N. C.
BLUMS' STEAM POWER PRESS PRINT.
1890.

# TWIN-CITIES OF NORTH CAROLINA.

## CHAPTER I.

### Distinguishing Characteristics.

The TWIN-CITIES of Winston-Salem, are situated in a rolling woodland country amongst the foot-hills of the Blue Ridge Mountains—about one thousand feet above the level of the sea. They are distant from Greensboro, on the Piedmont Air Line Railroad, the great highway of traffc and travel between New Orleans, Mobile, Atlanta, Washington City and New York, only twenty-nine miles, which is reached by a branch of the Richmond & Danville Railroad. This line has been extended thirteen miles westward to Rural Hall where it connects with the Cape Fear & Yadkin Valley Road, but whose objective point is Wilkesboro, thence to Bristol, Tennessee, opening up from there, a direct line to Cincinnati, Ohio, and the immense grain markets of the far West. The Roanoke & Southern has been completed to Walnut Cove, eighteen miles north, by way of Madison, and Martinsville to Roanoke, Va., connecting with Norfolk & Western, and Shanadoah Valley Roads. From Winston-Salem South, the road will be built to give a competing line to Charleston, Augusta and Atlanta.

Shut in from the outside world, with only one road connecting them with the great centres of trade, the necessity of other outlets has presented itself, and been crystallized during the past few years in the two latter enterprises which have interested their citizens sufficiently to invest large amounts of capital, the R. & S. being owned and controlled almost exclusively by stockholders of the two towns—presenting a showing of energy and substantial prosperity not excelled in the South.

The population of the TWIN-CITIES is estimated at fourteen thousand, at least five thousand being colored laborers in the tobacco factories of Winston, with between seven and eight hundred operatives in the cotton and wool factories, grist mills, iron works, planing and saw mills, &c., of Salem. The white people who are thus employed are sober, industrious and moral in the strict sense of the word, both sexes finding work at remunerative rates. They occupy neat residences near their business, which are rented at reasonable prices. Their employers are humane and considerate, and there is nothing of the oppression and suffering sometimes found amongst the working people of the North. There are also many white girls and women engaged in house service, and while they are efficient as help in kitchen and house, are respected by those who engage their services.

Both male and female colored hands are employed in the tobacco factories, women earning so much higher wages there, than in families as cooks and house-servants, that house-keepers find it difficult to procure steady help amongst this class of population.

There is very little lawlessness in their lives, as the police system of Winston is second to none in the United States, and yet strange to relate, quiet and industrious as they are, making good wages all the time, yet they spend money freely on dress and luxuries to eat, and save nothing, having little apparent ambition to secure for themselves homes of their own,—preferring to rent, and trust to the future with that happy complacency distinguishing the race.

Salem can boast of only one police-man which is all-sufficient, as no act of violence ever disturbs the quiet of the place, its inhabitants retiring at night with no fears of midnight intruders. There is no saloon within its limits, no gambling house to entrap the unwary, while the saloons of Winston are all relegated to the back and side streets.

Both places have a fine system of water-works, the water being pumped into reservoirs by means of overshot wheels from large wells and ponds in the vicinity, furnishing an abundant supply for every purpose. The first water-works were in operation in Salem in 1778, improved in 1828 and at subsequent periods since.

To the stranger, the contrast between the two places is very striking. Salem—representing the sturdy old civilization of years of toil and care, with a refinement of taste in all its surroundings, coupled with the common-sense durability of the works of the early

Moravian settlers, and the fresh enterprise, modern buildings and general air of the life of to-day in Winston. Strange to chronicle, lying as they do side by side, one only a continuation of the other, the difference only manifest by the marking of the streets, each with its separate city government, separate post-office, yet in no way the rival of the other, and both living together socially and commercially with the utmost feelings of fraternal regard and relationship,—nearly one hundred years stretching from the early settlement of the one to the foundation of the other.

Winston is known to the world as a great tobacco centre—Salem as the seat of the oldest female college in the South, and many do not recognize the fact, that the two are connected by the close ties that bind them together—or that Salem has the largest cotton and wool factories of the State, two fine grist mills, and saw and planing mills equal in capacity to anything in North Carolina.

The two towns recognize in each the help-meet of the other. Winstonians invariably drive visitors to the places of historic interest in Salem round which a tinge of romance hangs for all sight seers, and Salemites, in turn, show their guests through the large tobacco factories of Winston, and explain the immense business that throbs and pulsates through the marts of trade. They are proud also of showing its elegant stores; handsome churches and fine private residences—with its Macadamized Streets, courthouse square paved with square blocks of granite, and business houses built up compactly around the temple of justice, and stretching to the adjoining streets.

The climate is temperate, healthy and salubrious. Nestled at the foot of a chain of mountains, the country is exempt from those sudden changes of extreme heat and cold that characterizes many places. The water is a clear, pure, delicious freestone and very plentiful. In Salem is a fine spring of Chalybeate mineral water, prized for its medical qualities, and a resort for the citizens, but could be made available to strangers by a little outlay of money. At present, the water is only sold on the streets—delivered at the doors of residences. The elevation above the sea-level precludes the possibility of the existence of epidemics of yellow fever, and deaths from malarial disease are about one hundred to ten hundred. People live to a ripe old age, while deaths from consumption average only about five hundred to every ten thousand—intestinal diseases about one hundred and fifty to ten thousand. These figures indicate the advantages of Winston-Salem, as a healthy location for families—and the entire safety parents feel in sending their daughters to Salem to be educated. During so many years of the life of the noted educational institution and the thousands of girls sent here from malarial districts, very few have ever died.

Every variety of fruit grows well and matures finely in this locality—the Fruit Fair held last August in Winston disclosing the fact that many nurseries in this vicinity do a thriving business—pears and peaches attaining to as great perfection as in the famous lands of California—and apples as delicate in flavor as those of any Northern market. The dried fruit industry has quite a trade in its line, as much is shipped to other places. Also a cannery does here a good local business. Particularly is this section the home of the grape, great quantities of which are raised for home consumption, and also made into wine. As early as 1769 the abundance of wild grapes in the Wachovia Settlements suggested the manufacture of wine, nineteen hogsheads being made during that year. Ever since, the cultivation of grapes has been an important industry by improving the varieties. Much wine of delicious flavor is made every year, one gentleman* who has kept his wine vaults in Salem, exporting in 1869 ten thousand two hundred and sixty gallons of wine—North, South, East and West. He says: "A large grape grower in the United States could not supply the demand of his own wines, and filled his orders with North Carolina wines, which is proof enough to show that our wines are all right."

Every variety of vegetable grows well in this climate, and no day in the year, but they are offered for sale at the door, by the thrifty country people, who do a thriving business with their truck patches. They also bring in a quantity of butter, milk, and wild game ready dressed, making Winston-Salem a desirable place for the purchase of delicacies for the table, as only the butchers have a market in either town.

The minerals found in the county are mica, which glistens all over the earth, iron, manganese, asbestos and traces of gold.

The iron is quite abundant, while eighteen miles north, on the Roanoke & Southern Railway in Stokes County, is situated the Danbury Iron mines, "which are exceedingly rich in their deposit." Adjacent to these mines, lie the Dan River Coal Fields, "which is the only coal deposit in the State worthy of mention in the *Coal Trade*, a pamphlet published in New York, with the endorsement of United States Government officials."

* S. T. Mickey.

The forests of valuable timber surrounding Winston-Salem—embrace nearly every variety grown in North America. The yellow pine, ten varieties of oak, and hickory are the most utilized, the latter "useful in manufacture of spokes and handles of different kinds," the white oak into baskets, and other varieties and yellow pine, birch, cedar, walnut, &c., into lumber for building purposes. The brick is of superior quality, and endurable.

Winston is lighted by electric and incandescent lights. Salem by gas in its buildings and residences and oil lamps on the streets placed at regular intervals, as has been the custom for a great many years. Salem has its streets paved with cobble stones and brick pavements put down long before the memory of the oldest inhabitant.

Trim flower beds, well clipped hedges of box, a profusion of roses, climbing honey-suckle, Virginia creeper in neat gardens to the side of the houses of Salem present a quaint picture, many of the dwellings fronting directly on the street and porches overhanging the side-walks, some of which are covered with tile roofs, like many of the old houses in the French portion of New Orleans. Above all, stretch the mighty arms of the stately old elms which have lined the side-walks so many years, linking their branches in bower-like beauty above the streets, beckoning a welcome to the stranger as they nod and kiss in the balmy sunshine.

Main street extends through both places for a distance of over two miles. Cherry street in Winston is the most popular for residences, where modern architectural skill is displayed in the elegant homes, with grassy lawns, gay parterres of flowers and sparkling fountains suggestive of ease, comfort and refinement, sloping down into Salem in one unbroken line of beautiful surroundings.

Winston occupies a more elevated site than Salem, perhaps seventy feet, and on the heights beyond to the northwest, is plainly visible, "The Pilot" a solitary mountain some twenty miles distant, its rugged outlines distinctly seen in the clear atmosphere. Excursions to the Pilot are of frequent occurrence from both places, a recreation from every day turmoil to nature's soothing repose.

Pilot Mountain, Surry Co., N. C.

# SUNSET ON PILOT MOUNTAIN.

BY MISS E. A. LEHMAN.

["The Pilot" is an isolated mountain peak in Surry County, N. C., of very peculiar formation. It has a large castellated peak on the east side, and a smaller one just beyond, known familiarly as the LARGE and SMALL PINNACLES. The Large Pinnacle, which is 300 feet higher than the mountain proper, resembles a huge castle with long white Gothic windows, and those lighted up by the setting sun, present a unique and beautiful scene. The Indiams called it "THE PILOT" because it served to guide them homeward when hunting. The Blue Ridge begins the grand mountain scenery of Western North Carolina, and the Pilot stands as an outpost or fortress, guarding the approach to the wildest, most romantic scenery east of the Rocky Mountains. It stands "a sentinel to guard the enchanted ground."]

The shadows slanting westward, now assume
A hazy outline e'er the evening gloom
Engulfs and closely wraps yon rising moon.
The crimson flashes of the setting sun
Glow from the windows of the mighty dome,
As if the giant of the castle lighted up
His evening fires, and quaffed his evening cup.
Fantastic shadows flicker to and fro,
As fancy mist-wreaths, curling, come and go.
The grand old Pilot stands, majestic and sublime,
A kingly presence, frowning o'er the hills of time;
He reigned supreme, father of myriad rills,
When Judah's star arose on Orient hills;
He stood a dread ambassador to heaven from earth,
When morning stars sang chorals to her birth;
His purple shadows frowned o'er rocky dell
E're Tyre arose or Priam's city fell!
While Old World splendor faded into night,
Or New World forests hailed the dawning light;
He stood alone, a mighty beacon high,
Telling the weary wanderer "Home is nigh."

A hoary priest he sits—enthroned in state—
With sacerdotal stole and jewelled plate;
Ruby, carnelian, topaz, amethyst,
Jasper, chalcedony, and sardonyx,
Rich tints commingled, until, all aglow,
A violet splendor covered all below;
While far-up rocky steeps reflect the light,
And lambent tongue-flames leap from height to height.
Upon his castellated brow the evening star
Beams clear and bright, with glory from afar.
The mist-robed hills kneel to their great High Priest,
In dim confessional, from great to least;
And nature's choral anthem rings meanwhile
Through every woodland nook and forest aisle,
The wailing minor of the sad-voiced pines
"In Kyrie Eleison" sweetly chimes,—
Until the moon's soft benediction gently falls,
And night's dark mantle shrouds them in a pall.

The moon now beams queen regnant of the sky,
Assumes the sceptre which the sun lays by;
Orion leads the brilliant, starry host
With stately tread they climb the shining cope.
While, in the centre of this star-lit dome,
Thou stand'st oh Mount! grand, beautiful, alone.

The calm and restful strength thy presence gives
Imbues me with a new-born strength to live.
The everlasting hills! with soothing art,
E'er still the pulses of my restless heart,—
And I am raised from earth to heaven
By strength and calm endurace through thee given!

*Salem, N. C.*

## CHAPTER II.

### Who are the Moravians?

"The brethren of Moravia, are descendants of a people, who, like the Vaudois of Piedmont, never bowed to the Romish yoke, but may be traced through the Greek, directly to the Primitive Church. The year 1457 saw the commencement of the Protestant Episcopal Moravian Church (under the name of the United Brethren, or *Unitas Fratrum*)—which existed in Bohemia and Moravia more than fifty years before the Reformation. It received its episcopal orders at the request of the Synod convened at the village of Lhota, in 1467, from the hands of Stephen, Bishop of the Valdenses, a people, who, in the secluded valleys of the Alps, preserved their faith pure from the apostolic age downward. The succession followed on to Bishop Amos Comenius, for many years resident of Fulneck, Moravia, (whose well-earned fame induced the English Government in 1641 to urge his presence with a view to effect an improvement in the educational system of the universities and schools) and Jablonsky was enabled to transmit to the renewed Church of the Brethren the ancient episcopal ordination in Berlin in 1735—when David Niteshmann, first Bishop of the renewed Church was consecrated."

"When Martin Luther began his reformation in 1517 the Brethren of Bohemia and Moravia constituted a church of Reformers numbering at least two hundred thousand members, counting over four hundred parishes, using a hymn-book and catechism of its own, proclaiming its doctrines in a confession of faith, employing two printing presses, and scattering Bohemian Bibles broadcast through the land." From there, they had extended into Poland, establishing colleges and translating the Bible from the original into Bohemian.

Through a succession of trying persecutions at the stake, tortured at the rack, imprisoned in loathsome dungeons, they had decreased in numbers, and became disheartened, yet never entirely losing the precious seed of their faith.

Driven into exile, rather than "wear the chain of papal Rome, they broke the strong tie which fastened to home and country and sought a spot where they might worship God in scriptural purity. It was a hard struggle; it was no small sacrifice, but they made it, and turned their backs forever on the fields and dwellings, which had witnessed their pious worship, trusting in the Lord as their guide."

Led by the pious Christian David they reached Saxony in June, 1722 where they found the tolerance they desired, and a friend in Count Zinzendorf, upon whose estate they were offered an asylum, and where they began to build the town of Herrnhut, which soon became the rallying-point for the oppressed descendants of the Ancient Brethren in Bohemia, Moravia and Poland.

Count Zinzendorf was a German nobleman, educated at the University of Halle, a man of learning and deep research, a philosopher, poet and author. Becoming deeply imbued with religious fervor while a student, he yearned to extend the Kingdom of God throughout the waste places of the earth. Such was the man, whom the exiles found in Saxony, and such were the people who came to him—a large landed proprietor, for succor. Their history, their struggles—their faith made such an impression that he espoused their cause, soon became their leader, formulated a plan to revive the Church, introduced their ancient discipline and received their venerable episcopate, from the hands of Jablonsky one of its last survivors.

Developing a genius as great as Shakspeare in poetry, or Beethoven in music, he threw himself into the work of organization, preaching, exhorting, visiting Denmark, Sweden and many portions of Germany and France. Everywhere was he successful, except in the latter country, as during the days of the profligate Louis XIV the people had little use for a religion which brought them self-sacrifice.

In England and Scotland he hunted up the remnants of Ancient Brethren, strengthening their numbers, establishing missions and otherwise directing the extension of his church including emigration to America, and from Herrnhutt sending out a colony to Pennsylvania where a congregation was organized at Bethlehem in 1742.

Through his efforts and other intellectual Brethren in 1749, the British Parliament passed an act by which the *Unitas Fratrum* or Unity of Brethren was acknowledged as a Protestant Episcopal

Church. By this act, the free exercise of all their rights as a Church were secured to the Moravian Brethren throughout Great Britain and all its colonies, a privilege they did not enjoy fully in any other European kingdom.

Thomas Penn, proprietor of Pennsylvania, testified that the settlers in America had conducted themselves in such a sober, quiet and religious manner, making so many wise improvements in their colony, and the attention of persons in high standing in England being drawn by the knowledge of the purity of their lives in England, made it desirable to offer them further inducements for other settlements, in the new country. Invitations and offers came in greater numbers than they could accept for want of means and men.

Upon a conference of the Brethren, Count Zinzendorf decided to arrange for the purchase of ten thousand acres of land in North Carolina, owned by Lord Granville, and offered at a reasonable price. "Bishop Spargenberg who was well acquainnted with American affairs was sent in 1752 to reconnoitre the country, and act according to his judgment."

"Count Zinzendorf's idea was the following: He desired that his Brethren might not only have an opportunity to be of spiritual benefit to such persons as in process of time might settle in their neighborhood, as well as to gain access to various tribes of Indians, such as the Cherokee, the Catawbas, the Creeks, and the Chickasaws, but his main object was to acquire the possession of a larger tract of land where the Moravians might live undisturbed, having the liberty of excluding all strangers from their settlements. For this purpose it was resolved not to make the good qualities of the land the principal object, nor to buy detached parcels of the best land, but rather to select an undivided tract of about one hundred thousand acres. In the centre of this territory of the Brethren, a town was to be laid out containing the choir-house for single brethren, single sisters, widows, and the educational institutions. In this central place were also to be located a preparatory school for ministers and missionaries, and the directing board, for their outward and spiritual affairs in this, their own and independent country. Besides this one town, the rest of the territory was to be parcelled out to farmers belonging to the Church."

"There were three principles adopted by members of the Brethren's unity as the basis of their union—the Bible as the only source of Christian doctrine; public worship to be administered in accordance with the teaching of the Scriptures, and on the model of the Apostolic Church; and the Lord's Supper is to be received in faith, to be doctrinally defined in the language of the Bible, and every human explanation of that language is to be avoided."

One of their most learned English divines says: The name Moravian is one not assumed by ourselves, but so perseveringly applied to us by others, that we have been forced to adopt it as our distinctive denomination. But *Unitas Fratrum* is the name of our choice. The command of our Saviour: "Go unto all the world and preach the gospel unto every creature," is our maxim. As a missionary Church the world is our parish. We must have tabernacles in Christian lands that from such fixed spots we can direct and impel movements which aim at the whole world. To continue our vast missionary work we want to train suitable men; we want to interest others in our labors that they may, with a portion of their wealth, aid us to evangelize the earth."

Suffering so much from persecution in the past, the renewed church was averse to becoming involved in the politics of the countries in which they lived, and by the act of Parliament recognizing them as a church they were granted the privilege in Great Britain and all her colonies to be exempt from taking an oath, and instead of the usual form, permitted to make their solemn affirmation—which was to be received and considered as binding, in all the courts of justice as an oath from others Furthermore it was enacted "that they should be exempt from military duty, but be obliged to pay a certain tax in lieu of such services in proportion as that of others residing in the same colony, but this privilege was only extended to those bearing a certificate of church membership.

While contemplating the character of the early Moravians of North Carolina we are lost in admiration—here were a people seeking homes in a trackless wilderness, guiding their lives by Christ as a model, relying upon His strong arm in every hour of trial, seeking to be the first, true and faithful in order to impress others with the loveliness of the Christian beautitudes, proposing to educate the heathen and erect an altar for religion which should become a centre of missionary effort.

Stern and uncompromising as they may have appeared to outsiders, strict in the minor details of secular life, which were regulated by the tribunal of the Church, yet in every rite and ceremony there is an object lesson of the idealizing of patient cross-bearing, and a sublimity of heroism manifest, that gives each peculiar custom a significance that speaks with an unknown tongue to the innermost chords of deep feeling, and awakens strains typical of the glory-land above. We recognize the possibility of an earthly existence above the follies and vanities of the world, an attractive symmetry in all their methods, and a wisdom never excelled by the settlers in any other portion of the country.

---

## CHAPTER III.

### Settlement at Bethabara (Old Town).

The first Anglo-Saxons who ever set foot on American soil was a colony brought from England by Sir Walter Raleigh, which settled on Roanoke Island, North Carolina, in 1583. They looked for gold, and almost starved to death before being rescued by another English nobleman, who had made explorations on the Pacific coast and, returning, took them home in his ships.

Several years later, Raleigh made another attempt to effect a colony in Carolina, as Queen Elizabeth had given him large possessions, which he had named Virginia* in her honor,—but without success, his people only taking back tobacco and potatoes, and learning the English how to use them, as the result of all his vast expenditure of money and time.

After the English settlement at Jamestown, Va., had been effected, parties from there explored Carolina, and some few made settlements. In 1663, King Charles II. granted to eight of his favorite courtiers patents to "all that country between the Atlantic and Pacific Oceans, between 31 and 36 parallels of latitude, to be called Carolina in his honor. These noblemen for a long while appointed governors, and settlers began slowly to occupy the country, principally Germans and Swiss; but not more than ten thousand inhabitants were in the State in 1729. Becoming disgusted with the small revenues arising from their landed estates, and the trouble with their governors, who were sometimes just, sometimes oppressive, these proprietors decided to sell their claims to the crown, "receiving in return 2500 pounds sterling each." All accepted this proposition except Lord Granville, who determined to retain his eighth part, which was laid off for him, adjoining Virginia, in 1743.

* All the land from Nova Scotia to Florida was called Virginia.

This was the section which he was contracting to sell to the Moravians for their North Carolina settlement, and for which Bishop Spangenberg was appointed to make all necessary arrangements. Selecting five brethren at Bethlehem, Pennsylvania, they travelled on horseback for nearly a month until they reached Edenton, where they were joined by Lord Granville's surveyor-general. Striking out into the wilderness of Western North Carolina, they wandered for eight weeks among mountains and pathless forests, but did not find such tracts of land as they desired. "Following their compass eastward they reached the Valley of the Yadkin," and, accepting the hospitality of some white settlers, found what they had sought farther west, "a larger tract of rolling woodland, well-watered and suitable for their purpose." The surveyors commenced work, and Bishop Spangenberg and his companions returned to Pennsylvania, to report the result of their labor. They named the tract "Wachovia," because of the meadow (Aue) along the (Wach) principal creek, bearing some resemblance in its topographical outlines to a valley in Austria, formerly in possession of the Zinzendorf family. The brethren were not able to pay for these lands, so a land company was formed in England, and the purchase money was paid by subscription amongst the members and friends of the brethren, and the title deeds were given to "James Hutton, of London, Secretary of the Unitas Fratrum, to be held for the Church."

When Bishop Spangenberg reported what had been done, on his return to Bethlehem, preparations were at once set on foot to begin the new settlement, and twelve single brethren arranged to go permanently, accompanied by three others who were merely on a prospecting tour, expecting to return in a few months. Procuring a large wagon, drawn by six horses, they started on the long journey, through mountain passes, across rivers that had never been forded, with a stock of such articles as were needed on the trip and for use in the work which lay before them, in the wilds of North Carolina. Amongst them was a minister, Bernhard Adam Grube, who had been ordained in Germany, of which country he was a native. Another important character was Jacob Losch, born in New York, superintendent of the colony in temporal affairs. And another was Hans Martin Kalberlahn, a Norwegian, who had lived for years at Herrnhut, arriving in Bethlehem about one month before the emigrants left, cheerfully accepted the appointment as surgeon and medical adviser.

The nine other brethren were farmers and mechanics, mostly from Europe, representing the different trades, one being a tailor. The wisdom of these selections was afterwards manifest, all determined to help one another in the bonds of unity, but with the safe security of having each branch of industry needed to develop their plans thoroughly understood by at least one man in the colony.

After a varied experience of nearly six weeks, sometimes being compelled to unload their wagon and carry its contents over the mountains, sometimes going out of their route to thrash oats for their horses, they finally reached their destination, November 17th, 1753, where Bethabara, generally called Old Town, now stands.

Here they found shelter in an unoccupied cabin built by a German squatter, and abandoned some time before, thankful for even this scanty shelter, it being so small there was not room for them all to sleep. A hammock was suspended over the heads of the others for one of their number, and after a season of prayer and a lovefeast, they retired to rest, sensible of the fact that they were in a wilderness, as they listened to the howling of the wolves around their humble place of rest. The daily word of the Church, appointed for each day of the year, seemed very appropriate: "I know where Thou dwellest, even in a desert place"; and another, "Be ye of one mind." They accepted this as significant that God was following His children, and would guide them aright if they would cling together in the unity of love.

The next day was Sunday, so they found it quite a day of rest, and on Monday sharpened axes and hoes, and prepared to subdue the forests and fields of the future, beginning the construction of a bake-oven, and looking out for a mill to buy corn. They also selected eight acres that day to be cleared for the purpose of planting wheat, and were soon busy plowing, and in two weeks had seed sown for the crop. Preparations went on for the winter. One man was sent to bring salt from Virginia, another went to Dan River to buy oxen, and others were dispatched to the Yadkin to buy flour and corn. The fame of their wisdom and sagacity began to spread, and soon the Moravian doctor began to be known through travellers, who gave such praise to his skill and knowledge that many came to secure his medical attention, even at a distance of 60 miles. These services were paid for in provisions and stock, and was of material help to the settlers. Their tailor, too, became known, and very soon had work to do, deer-skins being sometimes brought in to make clothing. Unfortunately, they had no place for visitors, so another cabin was built, with a shed, for sleeping apartments; and thus the first winter was passed.

The next spring, John Jacob Fries succeeded Brother Grube, who was called North, as spiritual overlooker of the colony. He was born in Denmark, and was an accomplished scholar, especially in the Hebrew language, yet was not averse to a home in the wilderness if he could serve God and his fellow-man.

Bishop Boehler arrived soon after, and during his stay, the name Bethabara (house of passage) was given to the colony; still keeping in view, at a future day, the founding of a settlement in a more central location.

During the next fall their numbers were increased by seven men, led by a brother who came to superintend the construction of a mill. Their coming revealed the necessity for a larger house, and the corner-stone was laid, with great solemnity, in November, for the first building erected by Moravians in North Carolina. This was made large enough for a habitation of single brethren, and was dedicated by religious services being held by Bishop Nitschmann, who had come to visit the embryo town.

Twenty-three unmarried brethren and seven married couples soon arrived: a dwelling was built, a grist mill commenced and a meeting-house erected. Three months after, the married people moved into their new dwelling, the first child was born, and. in holy baptism, named Anna Johanna Krause. Others arrived from Pennsylvania and Europe, and at the close of 1756, the inhabitants numbered sixty-five persons.

The first difficulties of life in the forest having been overcome, everything had now a fair outlook. During the year 1755 the breaking out of war with the Indians,—called the "Old French war,"—gave them cause for disturbance. It had commenced in the colonies of the North, but gradually spread South. Ten brethren and sisters were murdered on the Mahoney, and it was deemed expedient to fortify the settlement by surrounding it and the mill with palisades, and became known throughout all the surrounding country as the "Dutch Fort." This fortification, rude in construction, was a place of refuge to many fugitives, even from distant portions of Virginia, where they found a safe retreat, plenty to eat, and an opportunity to attend religious worship.

Occasionally, companies of Indian warriors, Cherokees, Creeks and Catawbas, passed through the country and camped near by. They were given something to eat and treated kindly, and never committed any depredations. Sometimes they were accompanied by a British officer, or had a passport from the English Government. They were always received and fed, the government of North Carolina afterwards paying the Moravians for this, as, by their kindness, they saved the people from much disaster.

Bethabara was known, far and near, by the Indians, as "the Dutch fort, where there are good people and much bread." It is estimated that during 1757–'58 more than five hundred Indians passed through the settlement at various times. Because of the war, a famine prevailed in all the surrounding country extending into the districts of Virginia, and people came to Bethabara, more than a hundred miles, to buy flour and corn. The brethren had plenty to sell, as they had cleared and planted additional land, and had raised abundant crops. Some of the refugees decided to remain, captivated by the religious life of the people, and another settlement was decided upon, that of Bethania, which was laid off during the Summer of 1759.

The Indian war recommenced in October of the same year, and great was the anxiety concerning the safety of the two colonies. Brother Tosch was made captain of the Dutch fort, and had day and night watches at both places, directed by Bishop Spangenberg, who had arrived on an official visitation, and also couriers passed between both places, the high hill where the graveyard was situated at Bethabara serving as a fine lookout for all the surrounding country. Bishop Spangenberg also directed that the church bell should be rung each morning at dawn of day. Sometimes Indian tracks would be found outside the fort, and sometimes they played at ball along the meadow, but they never ventured nearer, and tradition tells us the ringing of the bell was the cause of their keeping a safe distance, unless upon friendly purposes intent. Their design of taking prisoners between the two places was also frustrated. They said: "The Dutchers had big, fat horses, and rode like the devil," scaring them from their acts of depredation. Outside the fort the people did not fare so well, fifteen being killed in the vicinity, one man coming into Bethabara with two arrows sticking in his body.

During the year 1761, by a simultaneous movement of the South Carolina militia, near Fort George, and troops from Virginia and North Carolina on the north, the Creeks were forced to sue for peace. The Brethren, being exempt from military duty, had remained at home, and supplied the troops with large quantities of flour from the Bethabara mill.

Next year, quiet being restored, another installment of settlers arrived from Pennsylvania, by way of Wilmington, bringing with them a small organ, the first in the colony, and a bell for the church at Bethania, only three miles away.

Thirty-five years after the first settlement, in 1788, the substantial church, still used as a house of worship, was built, which is a wonder to tourists who care enough about relics of the past to hunt it up, known as the church at Old Town, six miles distant from the Twin-Cities.

## A Visit to Old Town.

The road from Winston winds over an undulating country, past well cultivated fields, orchards bending beneath their loads of fruit, while in the distance the crags of the mountains are visible. The village of Bethabara, or "Old Town," lies in a peaceful valley, and only can be seen when the traveller reaches the eminence immediately surrounding. What a strange sensation of interest filled the soul as we slowly drove down the one street of the place, where there is little left now of the dwellings of a century and a half ago! Several old structures with stone basements, high porches and large rooms are still standing as a remnant of the old days and a dumb protest against the decay in which they have been allowed to fall; while nature, more merciful than man, seeks by mossy verdure and trailing vines to throw a veil of unspoken sympathy over the fragments where devoted lives wrestled with fierce difficulties, and where persistent labor conquered through years of trial and disappointment. From out the windows peeped little flaxen heads, strangely out of place in their tumble-down surroundings, attracted by the rumble of the vehicles, to look with wonder upon people from the outside world of which they know nothing. At either end of the long street is a handsome private dwelling, in modern style,—these and a railroad embankment about fifty feet in front, spoiling the prospect and disturbing to some degree the dream of the past.

In the centre of the village stands the wonderful old church, built of grey stone, with broad hall about twelve or fourteen feet wide, running through the centre, from which leads a staircase to the rooms above. One side of the hall is the place of worship; on the other are four living rooms for the minister and family. The church-yard is covered with a grassy carpet, and umbrageous shade trees invite repose, while the hill gradually slopes down in rear of the church to the meadow, certainly one of the most charming pictures of pastoral beauty, through which murmurs a clear stream, crossed by a rustic bridge. Beyond rises the hill where the graveyard is situated. We could well understand that minds appreciative of the beautiful in nature should have been fascinated by the surroundings, and impelled to make here the foundation for a new colony. At the corner of the church stands a stone monument, or rather slab, upon which is inscribed :

*Wachovia Settlement begun*
*17 November,*
*1753.*

This marks the spot where the little cabin stood, which the advance guard of the Moravians found and occupied until they could provide better quarters. High up on the end of the church is inserted a stone tablet,—

*Church built.*
*1788.*

With reverence we passed into the church built by pious hands, the stone quarried from the rocky beds near by, floors made of wide planks slick with the tread of many feet, hewn from forest trees. The walls are plastered and kept clean by whitewash, the windows, four in number, have deep embrasures, and are hung with wooden shades arranged with slats that open and close by pulling a cord. A stove serves to heat the building in winter. The benches have straight backs. The pulpit has a candle stand each side and a table in front with claw legs, while a high backed chair, carved by hand, with leather seat fastened down by brass tacks, all made of native walnut, completes the furniture of this quaint house of worship. A melodeon in the centre and kerosene lamps along the sides of the building, where the old candlesticks are still to be seen, are the only things of modern make within the walls. The choir gallery is to the right of the church, the railing carved with old-fashioned precision. An old trombone, one of the four used formerly in all Moravian churches, and some ancient music, together with a lot of old German books, are to be found in a small closet on one side of the gallery, which is lighted by two small windows, so arranged as to present the appearance of being diamond-shaped, when in reality there are only three panes of glass in each, let into a diagonal-shaped space becoming more angular as the inner edge of wall is reached. A few steps lead to the living rooms above and the tower from which hangs the same bell that frightened the Indians so badly when sounding the notes of alarm in the first meeting-house of Bethabara. In one of the rooms is a tall stove, made of embossed, earthen tiles, put together quite artistically, made here like those used at that time in the old country, and similar to one in the Virginia State Capitol, sent from England as a present to General Washington. From the church two large doors and windows, with sliding panels, open into the broad hall, where benches are arranged to accommodate the people if a crowd was present. A large, square, glass lantern hangs against the wall, and a tall, old-style clock served to warn the worshippers how time passed.

The living rooms of the minister have large windows, with deep window seats (the walls of the building are two feet thick), and fire-places across the corner of the rooms. The corner cupboards, wardrobe, presses and desk, with secret compartments, found in these rooms are all made of walnut and cherry, dove-tailed together with a nicety unknown to the fast age in which we live. Benches and split-bottomed chairs are also to be seen. On one of the cupboard shelves is a German Bible presented to Bethabara church by Bishop Spangenberg, and a tall communion cup, made of cut glass, with carved wooden cover. Here is also the old baptismal service, a small china pitcher of peculiar make, indented at the mouth, and a china bowl, same pattern. The method is to hold the head over the bowl and pour the water over it three times, in the name of Father, Son and Holy Ghost. The china mugs and waiters for the Lovefeasts are stored in one of the presses of an adjoining room. The kitchen, with dressers, sinks, tables and benches, made of oak, has a bake-oven attached, with huge open fire-place, where a cord of wood could be burned at one time. A swinging crane, hanging within, brings back a suggestion of how the culinary department was managed under the old *regime*. The floor of this kitchen is laid with blocks of stone, and the whole a marvel of convenience for those times. These rooms are not used now— only the furniture preserved with care,—the minister preferring to live elsewhere. No portico or vestibule adorns the outside of church, only an entrance over large, irregular blocks of stepping-stones.

Several long benches under the locusts indicated the practice of the steady old members who sat there before the service began, discussed neighborhood news, told of letters from distant friends which came perhaps only semi-annually, and made plans for useful guidance amongst the people, regulating their lives by the line and plummet of the Bible. Coming in methodically at the ringing of the bell, the males all on one side of the church, females on the other, and children together on the low front benches, next the pulpit, under the eye of the minister,—they were seated with the utmost quiet prevailing, all joining in the hymns, led by the minister, no hapless urchin ever daring to raise his tiny hand to misbehave. Obedience was the watch-word of every life, instilled by precept and example at an early age.

Beyond the meadow a winding road leads up a steep hill, covered with ferns and mosses in the undergrowth, while above tower the giants of the forest, where the breeze sings a soothing threnody, wrapping the senses in a dreamy mist of sentiment and romance. At the top of this hill, which is about one hundred and fifty feet in height, an enclosure leads into the oldest Moravian graveyard in North Carolina, kept in a state of perfect preservation by the Church: each grave in shape with small stone lying flat upon the head of the grave, with name, age, death and some Biblical inscription. These are made of the sand-stone, and have become discolored with age, but the dates are perfectly legible. The oldest was buried in 1754. Bluegrass, clover and periwinkle spread a covering of green above the heads of the faithful, who rest in silence far from their native land.

In the centre of the middle walk stands a granite monument, about fifteen or twenty feet in height; erected near the remains of a famous missionary from Germany, who came to the settlement and died here, after an arduous life among the Esquimos and inhabitants of different portions of the globe. This was placed here in 1888, the services celebrating the centennial of the building of the church.

*In Commemoration*
*of*
*Moravian Missions Among*
*the Heathen.*
"*They that sow in tears, shall reap in joy.*"
MATHEUS STACH.
*Here lies buried the body of the first Moravian*
*Missionary to Greenland.*

We quietly stole away down the zig-zag path, entered our carriage and came back to busy life with the words of the poet ringing in our ears :—

"Here peace divine o'er glimmering grove and grass,
Hallows the sunshine in the noon's warm lull;
Ethereal shadows gently pause, or pass,
Flecking with gold the hill-slope beautiful."

GRADED SCHOOL, WINSTON, N. C.

## CHAPTER IV.

### The Guardian Angel.

Among the early settlers of North Western North Carolina, about the year 1755, was a little colony of Moravians from Germany and Pennsylvania. Accustomed to the colder winters of the North, these good people were delighted with the mild climate of the Sunny South, which as late as December was often as balmy as the early Autumn.

These hardy people had settled, built a village, Bethabara, surrounded it with a stout stockade to prevent a surprise from the Indians, and for general security in the wilderness. Every improvement bore the marks of their German taste. Inside the fortifications were grouped the queerest cottages, with steep roofs, sometimes extending far over and making a kind of porch, all built of the stoutest material. The doors were cut in half, and swung on separate hinges, so that one could be closed, leaving the upper half open for ventilation, while the closed lower half was a kind of protection from sudden intrusion. Separate houses were built for business purposes, for in the usual German management, the necessary trades were represented and conducted under the supervision of a warden ; while the spiritual supervision was conducted by the pastor and board of elders. Outside the fort were the farms, the proprietors all living in the village. Thus, in a quiet orderly manner, these people were in fact a little community, governed by a board of trustees—all living happily together, increasing their resources as their wants demanded.

On one of those bright autumnal days which often linger as late as December, even reaching the Christmas holidays, a group of bright children were playing outside the "palisades." The busy wives were engaged in spinning or weaving and some gossiping with neighbors, leaning over their half opened doors in the enclosed village. One of the children called out, "Let's get permission to go to the hill-side"—and with a rush they entered the village, and obtaining their wish were soon racing across the meadow to the fern-clad hill beyond. In the fields the men were at work, their guns near by, as in the forest beyond lay the "war-path" of the Cherokee Indians where they passed to attack the Indians of Virginia. The day was indeed beautiful; the birds were singing in the hedge-rows, and coveys of partridges rose in their short flight amongst the stubble. The older boys of the village were up the hill after evergreens, for it was near Christmas time, and every cottage must have its tree, and the church must be decorated for the season. The girls, meanwhile, were busy gathering the luxuriant ferns and moss, singing cheerful songs. Towards evening, the boys came down loaded with cedar boughs; others came with laurel, gathered from more distant hills, drawn on rude sleds—all singing merrily and joining the girls, they moved homeward—all but one—a little girl the pride of the village and pet of the household. Always gay and full of life she had wandered farther round the hill, attracted by stray creepers of trailing evergreen pine, and the lovely ferns which seemed to grow larger as she crept along the slope—not thinking of her companions—Bunch after bunch was discarded, for apparently better specimens, until the deepening shadows caused her to turn to find her companions gone out of hearing—all was silent in the deep damp bordering the wood. She was way beyond the path. Gathering up her treasures, she turned as she thought homeward, but no familiar land-mark was found, and she was about to call, when she felt a slight touch on her shoulder that startled, yet stopped her intended cry—a swaying cedar twig seemed to be the cause of the touch. Restless and uneasy, yet she really felt no fear, only anxious to get home. She moved on, and again a sharper touch nearly turned her round, and again a cedar bough seemed the cause, and she pushed on at a more rapid speed, the darkness becoming deeper and the heavy undergrowth almost impassible, yet she hoped soon to reach the meadow and see the lights of the town. She knew she was lost, yet felt strangely calm and fearless. Every once and a while she seemed to be touched, and once so strong, she sat down on a log and burying her face in her hands—prayed silently. The moon now arose, and the forest shades were brighter. All at once a strangely human cry aroused her, and rising up she was about to answer when a sudden touch almost sent her prone to the ground. She quickly arose and a lowering cedar limb swayed to and fro. She thought again she had been struck by it.

She was now almost ready to drop with fatigue, yet that strange confidence kept her silent. Sitting down, she thought she heard the patter of little feet and sprang up only to be rudely, as she thought, forced into a circular cedar brake, like an arbor in a well-kept park. Here the cry again came, yet a touch again kept her quiet, and gradually completely overcome by fatigue she went to sleep. Again the shrill cry aroused her, and when about to answer a bright light surrounded and a gentle touch silenced her. This time she was startled, yet the moon-light caused her to think she might have been mistaken in both the halo and the touch. She again fell asleep.

In the village all was confusion and distress when the loss of the child was discovered. Wild with grief, the children told their story. They thought she had returned with the boys who brought the laurel, among whom was her brother—but not being found the men of the settlement started out, headed by her father and scattered through the forest with lighted torches.

The father and three others went to the mill, thinking perhaps she had gone there, as she had friends residing near by. Failing to find her, the almost demented father turned to the hill amongst the cedar brakes. They had scarcely turned before the fearful cry rung out on the night air. They knew, but two well what it meant, and with a heart-rending exclamation the father staggered and fell across a fallen tree. On recovering he urged to go on, for he too felt a strange comfort, but the others expected to find the child dead. Upon entering an open space of the forest a treacherous panther was seen stealing along the edge of the wood; and finally leaped out in the bright moon-light. Intantly three rifles rang out, and the animal dropped in his track dead.

All pushed on as soon as assured the panther was dead. Led by a guiding hand they came to a clump of cedars. The father noticed the singular shape, intuitively parted the boughs and there on the ground found his darling asleep. With a wild cry of joy, he hugged the startled child to his bosom, and with a thankful prayer in his heart, bore her out to his companions, who all sank on their knees and thanked God for his merciful care of the little one. The faith of the brethren was strong—the first they did was to remember their Lord and Master who had wrought this miracle.

The little one related her story as the happy parent bore her home. It was a considerable distance, and ere they were clear of the forest nearly day-break. The father told her it was her Guardian Angel who had touched and kept her quiet, and gave her the necessary strength to go on, until the cedar grove was found, and then she was allowed to sleep in peace. The good brethren broke forth in songs and thanksgiving as they approached the hill-side. The villagers heard the song and knew by the hymn tune that the child was found. The mother was out in the meadow first, followed by the good pastor and the people, and there, in the open meadow, in the early morning, the mother clasping her child to her breast, the whole congregation kneeled while the good pastor returned thanks to God for all His goodness. All sang the hymn of praise as they returned home.

The day after was Christmas, and the people gathered in the little church and enjoyed a happy and heart-felt love feast, strengthened in their faith as the pastor read the narrative of the lost child, as nearly in the simple child-like words given him by the little one. A visible emotion agitated every face, and when the little tapers were given to the children, as is the Moravian custom, all was brightness. The Christmas anthem was sung with unusual fervor, and it really seemed as if the Christ-child had indeed hovered over the village. B. T. E.

## CHAPTER V.

### The Founder of Salem.

Frederick William Marshall, who had been appointed Superintendent of the Wachovia settlement in 1763, was an intellectual, scholarly man, of great administrative ability. His father, an officer in the Saxon army, had given him a fine military education. While a student at the University of Leipzig, he met Count Zinzendorf, determined to study the English language and enter the Unity of the Brethren, hoping for a wide field of Christian usefulness. This man is known as the founder of Salem, and to his genius and taste the inhabitants are indebted for the location and improvement of the surroundings. He personally superintended the laying out and planting of cedars in the Avenue and graveyard, which are a wonder to all strangers ; so classic in their perfection that one marvels at the work of one hundred and twenty-four years—a monument that touches the tenderest chords of feeling. Beneath those fringed cedars his remains crumble into dust, but as long as they wave above his lowly grave, remain a perpetual reminder of him who spent a large private fortune to assist in building the church and making Salem attractive to the eye as well as noted for thrift and industry,—all dedicated to the service of Him he daily worshipped.

Early in 1765 he decided to locate the central town and selected the site, giving it the name Salem (peace), which had been chosen by Count Zinzendorf before his death. The ridge was surveyed, the square laid out, and a permanent settlement decided upon, deviating from the original plan which placed the church in the centre of the town, with streets radiating in every direction,—arranging it in parallel lines, to intersect at right angles.

In February, 1766, four new arrivals from Europe and four residents of Bethabara moved to the new place, felling the logs to build a hut in the woods. In June the first family house was built, and a loom set up. They increased in numbers, their oppressed brethren in Europe joining them very rapidly, and soon became very prosperous from their wise management. Everything was governed by agents of the Church, the hotel, bakery, provision store, tannery, saddlery, shoe-shop, and every class of labor—held in community; the Church paying them only a *pro rata* for their services. The lands were leased for farming purposes. Henry George himself would have envied the harmony of the working of this community of interest. No outsider was permitted to live within the Moravian settlements, and no reckless character, like those who often invaded the precincts of other places, ever disgraced the town by lawlessness. Their meeting-house bell awoke the inhabitants to their daily toil and duty, and sent them to bed at night with methodical regularity.

This combination of labor and harmony enabled them to accomplish wonderful results. Individual emolument was not thought of,—only the grand good of the whole community considered. Saw and grist mills were built, a system of water-works arranged. A bell was brought for the church, serving also as a town clock, and an organ with two stops took the place of the trombones brought from Europe in 1765. The first of the substantial brick buildings, now seen in Salem, was the Brothers' House, which is now known as the Widows' House. This was erected as a home for unmarried brethren of the Church. The lower rooms were used as a meeting-house on one side of the hall, other church offices below, while above was the dormitory, and the basement as kitchen, &c. This was used as a temporary place of worship until 1771.

when a congregation-house was built which was afterwards removed to make room for the main building of the Academy, the brethren's house being afterwards discontinued. The Revolutionary struggle was a time of great trouble to the Moravians. Having been allowed to hold their views about not bearing arms and taking oaths, they were sometimes subjected to many disagreeable indignities. They were permitted to pay the double tax as to the English government, but this was hard as corn and other provisions were very high and Continental money worthless. There was also some anxiety about the title to the lands, which had been transferred from James Hutton in London to Frederick Marshall, who was absent in Europe. When the "Confiscation Act of 1777" was passed by North Carolina, a clause of the title. "given in trust for the Unitas Fratrum", made it apparent that the act could not be extended to Moravian lands. They were only required to affirm their allegiance to the United States and pay the tax.

Frederick Marshall returned and wisely directed them through the trying days of the war. Sometimes the Continental, sometimes the British, travelled through the settlements entailing many losses upon the people. At last peace was declared after Cornwallis' surrender, whose whole army passed through Salem en route to Virginia.

The first fire-engine ever brought to America was received at Salem from Germany in 1785. During this year was built the Sister's House, still standing, a commodious brick edifice of two stories, some twenty-five rooms, one of the most quaint and substantial buildings, covered with tiles. The house is supplied with water and other conveniences, and kept in repair by the interest from a sum acquired when the spinsters of the Church all worked together and placed their earnings in a common fund. This has been discontinued some forty years, but the unmarried sisters still rent rooms there, who prefer not to live with relatives. The house of the brethren was taken for a Widows' House, managed exactly as the other, on opposite sides of the Public Square. If unable to pay nominal rent it is given them by the Church, but there are few who have not by frugality or inheritance a competency to provide for old age. It is very respectable to have a home in either house.

The facts about the Moravian Sisters are not generally understood—as even so great a poet as Longfellow in his poem, "Hymn of the Moravian Nuns at the Presentation of Pulaski's banner" got matters mixed. Miss Lehman, editor of the *Academy*, says:

"Pulaski, the gallant Pole, who came over to assist in the Revolutionary War, was at Bethlehem, Pa., on wounded furlough. Before he left the place the Moravian sisters (not nuns) presented him with a crimson banner, which he courteously accepted, saying it should be defended with his life, and be his shroud in death. The minor details of the poem are incorrect; there are no Moravian nuns, and the accessories of burning incense in swinging censers before the altar, the cowled heads, the nuns' sweet hymn, sang low in the dim, mysterious aisle,—all existed only in the poet's imagination."

## CHAPTER VI.

### Buildings and God's Acre.

The new Academy building was erected on the site of the old Congregation House joining the old Academy building on one side and connected with the church by a covered passage-way on the other during the year 1854. The main building alone presents a front of one hundred feet—opening directly on the street from the broad portico built in the Doric style of architecture—four stories in height—a massive pile constructed of pressed brick. There are north and south wings, broad halls, well ventilated rooms, "by means of trunk ventilators, four of which run up from the lower floor, extending above the roof. From these trunks, the different rooms are connected by branches." The buildings are supplied with gas and water throughout, and heated by large wood stoves, providing an even temperature during severe weather.

This seat of learning, the pride of Salem, has a peruliarly interesting history, having maintained itself since 1802, without a single endowment from any source.* The sole property of the Moravian church, it is managed by a Board of Trustees who have sought not to have it a money-making concern, but rather a sonrce of usefulness in preparing young women to fill their positions in life, with credit to themselves and families. Recognizing, first in

* Mr. F. H. Fries bestowed a gift of one thousand dollars to the Art Department in memory of his infant daughter who died several years ago known as the "Louise Memorial." Mr. H. E. Fries made a valuable donation to the Library, and a gentleman from Tennessee made also a similar gift, but no special Chair has ever been endowed.

the South, that to bring a nation to the highest point of civilization, there must be an educated, refined womanhood, the early Moravians bent all their energies in that direction, and their efforts have been abundantly successful. Beginning the boarding school, with eight pupils, they advertised their project of having a school where the home-life would be followed as closely as possible, together with strict discipline, thorough teaching and practical instruction.

They cherished for years the scheme of an educational missionary effort for the benefit of women, but nearly half a century passed away before any active steps were taken, and the corner-stone of the Academy was laid with religious ceremonies.

The people of the South responded to the call for students, and sent their daughters for instruction from distant portions of the country—in carriages, by stages, even in ox-wagons, before there was a railroad anywhere in the United States.

At least ten thousand *Alumni* claim this as their *Alma Mater*—comprising some of the most distinguished ladies of the South, who have gone forth to shed an influence upon society, second to none in the nation. Amongst them two who have been called upon to do the honors of the White House—Mrs. President Polk and Mrs. Patterson, daughter of President Jackson. Mrs. Gen. Stonewall Jackson and Mrs. Gen. D. H. Hill were also educated here. Mrs. Polk, now living in seclusion in her Tennessee home, sends an occasional letter to the Academy paper, breathing her love and veneration for the school of her youth with messages of encouragement to the teachers who have succeeded those of her day and generation.

Even during the late civil war the school flourished ; as parents sent their daughters here for a safe retreat, knowing that evil would befall them less likely than elsewhere. When Stoneman's raiding party entered Salem, the Mayor immediately surrendered, and together with the President of Academy asked that a Federal guard be stationed around the building for protection. This was granted, and teachers and scholars pursued the even tenor of their way unmolested. The broad front doors of the Academy are seldom opened except on grand occasions, as visitors are received at the President's house, but in the rear is one of the most beautiful parks to be found anywhere. Wide spreading weeping willows bending over large fountains, broad sweeping walks, terraced hills, cozy little dells, attractive pagodas shaded by Norway spruces, and other trees more than a hundred years old, form one artistic blending of taste and beauty.

The church, joining the Academy, is large and elegant* in its proportions. With its frescoed walls and ceiling, its pipe-organ of thrilling tone built in 1799 while the church was being constructed, its carvings of wood, wide galleries, and the deep silence, that broods over the congragation at all times, drawing the thoughts to the divine and bowing each head in reverance while the music steals upon the senses as a glimpse of some bright upper sphere, where the "*Gloria in Excelsis*" is forever the song upon every lip.

Two blocks beyond the church lies the Avenue, over a quarter of a mile in extent, and about one hundred feet in width. Along its outer edge were planted about twenty feet apart tall cedars more than one hundred years ago, and through its centre runs a broad gravelled walk about eight feet wide. The rest of the space is turfed, and as the walk follows the natural undulations of the land, is a most delightful place to spend a leisure hour, while happy children gambol amongst the grassy glades, and their elders drink in the fresh air enjoying the repose provided so thoughtfully by their forefathers. No vehicle is ever allowed within the gates of this avenue.

The Moravian grave-yard lies all along the right of this avenue, entered by three large gates—bearing above their arched entrances the inscriptions: "Blessed are the dead which die in the Lord," "Because I live ye shall live also," "Them also which sleep in Jesus will God bring with Him."

The grave-yard is laid off at right-angles, and planted with cedars. Where the walks intersect in the centre, four of these immense trees stand like sentinels above the first grave ever made in the place in the plot adjoining—bearing date 1771. At this spot the members of the church congregate on Easter morning, and hold a religious service, typical of the resurrection, with music from a band of six instruments—accompanying the singing of sacred anthems. The graves, green hillocks lying side by side, are provided with a stone lying flat upon the head of the grave, and decorated the evening before with various floral designs, and there can scarcely be imagined a more beautiful ceremony in the early morning, when the sun is first peeping above the tree tops of the distant forest.

The females are buried together, the males together, and the children have their own allotted place. According to custom, no costly stone is allowed within the enclosure, and no grave is unpro-

* Baptismal and Communion Service of solid silver.

vided for, the church keeping this spot, known as "God's Acre," in perfect order which is beautiful by its neat uniformity.

Beyond, lies the cemetery, owned by stockholders, for those who prefer burying families together, and where the people of Winston also bury their dead.

The grounds are reached by a rustic bridge spanning a ravine, and are laid off with some attention to modern landscape gardening; the sections sold to individuals. Some of the monuments are handsome, with two private vaults above one of which stands a life-size marble figure of Hope guarding the entrance.

Six graves in a paled enclosure has a stone bearing the inscription: "Our Confederate Dead." Soldiers who died in a hospital.

When a death occurs in Salem the announcement is made by the blowing of six brass horns in the church steeple, and the tune played indicates the age of the deceased. The body of the dead is never carried into the church where the services are held, but rests on a bier on the outside, in former days deposited in a small house at the rear of the church. Preceded by the horns, blowing some mournful dirge, the bier made of carved mahogony, is bourne on the shoulders of pall-bearers, and followed on foot by relatives and friends of the departed, one of the most touching funeral processions that can be imagined.

Between the grave-yard and Academy grounds lies Wachovia Park—a beautiful tract of forest land, spring of pure water, and a clear rippling stream murmuring over a pebbly bed—one of nature's choice uudisturbed spots of loveliness.

## HOW OFT I'VE TROD THAT SHADOWY WAY.

Full many a peaceful place I've seen,
But the most restful spot I know,
Is one where thick, dark cedars grow
In an old graveyard cool and green.

The way to the sequestered place
Is arched with boughs of that sad tree,
And there the trivial step of glee
Must sober to a pensive pace.

How oft I've trod that shadowy way,
In by-gone years,—sometimes while yet
The grass with morning dew was wet,
And sometimes at the close of day,

And sometimes when the summer noon
Hung like a slumberous midnight spell,
Sometimes when through the dark trees fell
The sacred whiteness of the moon.

Then is the hour to wander there,
When moonlight silvers tree and stone,
And in the soft night wind is blown
Ethereal essence subly rare.

At such an hour the angels tread
That hallowed spot in stoles as white
As lilies, and in silent flight
They come and go till dawn is red.

JOHN HENRY BONER.
Native of Salem, now of New York.

# CHAPTER VII.

## Peculiar Customs.

One of the peculiar customs of the early Moravians was that of marriage by lot. According to their ideas, young people were not allowed to mingle freely together in social life. There was no visiting or meeting except in the presence of their elders, after the European style. The young brethren lived together, and the young sisters, when fourteen years of age, left their homes and went to the Sisters' House, where they were under the guidance of an elderess of the Church, who directed what kind of employment should engage their attention in the various industries in which the sisters were proficient.

This was their home, as an increasing family in the paternal dwelling did not allow room or time for such study and reflection as was needed to fit them for the duties of life. When a brother desired to marry, he went to the pastor of the church, signifying his purpose, and perhaps naming the young lady whose character from reputation would suit him. Assembling the elders, after consultation and prayer, the matter was decided by lot, believing if it came out "yes" it was God's will, and if "no" accepting it as not the best for either they should live together in holy matrimony. When the lot revealed "yes," then the minister went to the elderess of Sisters' House and told her the decision. She summoned the young sister, who had the privilege of declining or accepting the offer of marriage after due consideration. If she accepted the day was appointed, and the elderess immediately set to work to help her prepare for the important event, one of the requirements being a goodly supply of linen for household use, which was spun from the flax cultivated so extensively in the country, and woven by their own hands. The marriage was usually celebrated at the church, the bride entering one door with her father, the bridegroom the other,—meeting at the altar perhaps for the first time.

The Synod of 1817 decided to abolish marrying by lot, some of the younger members rebelling against its requirements, as according to the Church discipline, if a brother went in opposition to the lot, he was immediately expelled, and not allowed to live in the settlement. There is no criticism of the custom. The matter was entered upon religiously, and accepted in faith, no evil consequences ever followed, and no divorce to this day has ever been known amongst the Moravians of Salem. Marriage has always been with them a sacrament, not a civil ceremony.

Their children are considered a part of the Church, not merely Sunday School scholars. Very early they are learned to attend the public services, and each has his hymn-book and reads the litany and engages in singing, presenting a uniformity of worship not found elsewhere. In the homes the daily text is read at the morning meal from a small pamphlet arranged yearly for each day in the year, with some verses from the Bible, one of which is always doctrinal. This is printed in different languages, and in use by Moravians all over the world. The children are also learned at an early age to ask the blessing at the table.

The Festival days are an important branch of church services—divided into the Sisters, Single Brethren, Widows, Married People and Children, when each class is thus honored, while at Christmas, Easter and other appointed days, the whole congregation unites in the celebration. The festival day is ushered in by music from the church steeple by the horns, chapel service in the morning, and in the afternoon a love-feast of sweet buns and coffee handed on trays by six gentlemen and six ladies, the latter with snowy dress caps and white aprons. The coffee is served in china mugs with milk and sugar already prepared. While partaking of this, the choir renders some fine anthems alternating with hymns by the congregation, only the music and swell of the organ through a continuous service with prayer at the opening and benediction at close comprising the features of the entertainment.

On children's day, after the love-feast in afternoon, there is a special programme for the night. Wires are stretched between the church and President's house with a symbolic figure in centre, and upon these are hung dozens of Chinese lanterns. When lighted, the children march out on the steps of the church, while the congregation passes through the side doors, and surround them while they sing a hymn led by the cornet. This is one of the most interesting occasions that can be imagined. The quiet hush of the night, the myriad of stars twinkling in the firmament above, the varying brilliant lights, the sweet voices of children raised in praise to "Jesus lover of my Soul"—all must fasten the scene upon a child's imagination never to be erased. The decorations of flowers inside the church, and designs for lanterns outside are different every year.

On Christmas eve the church is beautifully decorated, one of the attractions being an exquisitely painted transparency, representing the "mother and child," the light so arranged as to throw a halo around the head of the infant Christ. During the services, wax candles, about four inches in length, are passed on trays, then lighted, one is given to each child, emblems of the light which Christ brought into the world. As they pass from the church with their twinkling lights, the scene is picturesque and attractive with its speaking symbolism.

The last night of the year the church is generally crowded and two services are held, at eight and half-past eleven. During the first the "Memorabilia" are read—an epitome of important events all over the world and especially the congregation during the year. When the clock sounds out the first stroke of twelve suddenly the congregation rises in the midst of the speaker's remarks, by one mighty impulse supported by the church band and sing rejoicingly the hymn, "Now let us praise the Lord." Then they are dismissed amidst the wishes and congratulations of "Happy New year."

Out from this refining atmosphere have gone forth to other localities, young men who have made themselves known in the world of thought and labor—many occupying positions on the leading journals of the country, New York, Washington, the West and *Texas, bearing evidence of their correct training while the musicians from Salem, male and female, have been distinguished for their genius displayed in the leading cities of the Union. West Point and Annapolis had their cadets from Salem who are now officers in United States Army and Navy, amongst the "bravest of the brave" in point of personal courage.

## CHAPTER VIII.

### The Old Salem Hotel.

The old Salem Hotel is a place of interest to strangers, by virtue of the tragedies that have occurred beneath its roof, and the fact that a veritable ghost was said to have made its appearance there, more than half a century ago, and other items of historical importance.

The first inn which occupied the same site was burned in 1784, and the hotel was built the same year. It was leased to parties who were required to sign a written document pledging themselves "to be agreeable and polite to all strangers, to keep an entirely clean and inviting House of Entertainment—to watch the domestics carefully that they may be polite and obliging and not demand any extra gratuity, and in case they were found guilty of asking for money, to dismiss them without ceremony. They were also required "not to allow gambling, fighting, swearing, immoral conduct or the assembling of minors on Sundays, or to permit the use of spirituous liquors to persons intoxicated or any excess of drinking on the premises."

"The tavern," as it was familiarly termed, thus conducted became the social centre of the town. It was the customary resort of the burghers, who regularly congregated about the large fire-place of the public room in winter or on the long veranda in summer to discuss the affairs of the place, and general news of the day as they smoked."

After the Academy became a success, examination day was the great event of the year. As there were no railway facilities the wealthy Southern planters came in elegant coaches with a train of colored servants and fine horses—the like of which has never been seen since the civil war. "The large hotel yard was literally packed with carriages. It would be difficult to describe those times when Southern aristocry was at its zenith, and nowhere else at that time could be found so great a collection of wealth, beauty, all the courtly graces and chivalric bearing which characterized Southerners in ante-bellum days.''

The buildings are four in number. ''The large red brick are of immense size, the walls as thick as a feudal castle and the queer saddle roof with dormer windows was surmounted by a cupola and bell. The chimneys had great immense fire-places, the kitchen paved with blocks of stone. The property was afterwards purchased and kept for years as a place of entertainment for man and beast, but is not now used as a hotel—the rooms being rented in suits. Thus the glory has departed from its attractive history much to the regret of the travelling public who were always sure of welcome and comfort as long as it held out its arms to strangers.''

Half a century ago, so the story goes, a gentleman came to this hotel and registered under an assumed name. The proprietor was kind and pleasant. He was sick, and in a day or so was found to be afflicted with the small-pox, and was removed to a house on the edge of town and a nurse provided.

He became worse and sent for the proprietor of hotel when found he must die, who did not reach him before death claimed him as a victim. The old gentleman was greatly troubled and for days wondered who he was, and whence he came. Soon afterwards, one of the female servants complained while cleaning the room he had occupied at hotel that his face had appeared to her. The proprietor scolded her for such superstition—but after repeated shrieks of fear and declarations that he was really present, he decided to investigate for himself. The uncanny visitor met him within the threshold of the room, told his real name and place of residence and desired his wife should be apprized of his death, disappeared and has never since been seen. The grave old Moravian, pale and collected, would not tell his strange experience, but wrote to the address named, received a reply from the wife and sent all his effects home. 'Tis said the old gentleman never liked to talk about the incident, which he declared to be literally true.

The Widows' House had its ghostly visitant also, in the person of a workman who was killed by a rock crushing out his life while excavating for its cellar. He was attired in red shirt and skull-cap, and one of the inmates of the building, long years afterwards declared she met him on the stair-case. This legend of the ''Little Red Man'' was written up for the *Century* several years ago, the author's mother then occupying rooms at the Widows' House. None of the present inhabitants have ever seen him and refuse to believe the superstition, but still they like to tell the story to the curious who are fond of turning over the dust of years and peeping into past mysteries.

There was a European chemist who drifted to Salem and took up his abode at the hotel, bought property, planted an orchard and vineyard, and made himself at home amongst the people—though reticent about his former history. One evening in 1857, while making some chemical experiments a terrific explosion occurred in his room which tore through the walls, shattered the windows, flung the piano in the adjoining parlor across the room, and killed the experimenter, mangling him terribly. His burial in the dusk of the evening, coupled with the circumstances was very impressive.

A gentleman from a distance while sick and suffering from temporary mania, or by design, during the absence of his attendant, threw himself from the second story window of his room and was instantly killed. This winds up the pitiful list of tragedies that tell of the strange complications of human lives.

"It was to this hotel that Peter Stuart Ney, supposed by many to have been Napoleon's Marshal Ney, of France, used to come while he resided in Davie county in 1840 or '41, and attracted crowds who stared in open-mouthed wonder at his thrilling feats of sword play, and other martial exercise.

There is also a room held sacred, where General Washington slept during his stay in Salem.

Some of the modern private residences of Salem are pictures of beautiful comfort with their smoothly shorn lawns, groups of statuary, urns filled with trailing plants, large ivy-covered buildings of substantial structure—all surrounded by the mystic halo of contentment.

FIRST FIRE-ENGINE BROUGHT TO AMERICA.

## CHAPTER IX.

### Settlement of Winston.

During the year 1848, the old county of Stokes was divided by Act of Legislature, and a new county formed, naming it Forsyth, in honor of Colonel Benjamin Forsyth, an Indian fighter, who was killed in Canada in 1814, a native of the older county.

The seat of justice was selected where now stands the town of Winston, and the following year the Moravian brethren of Salem sold fifty-one acres in the woods beyond their town for that purpose, at five dollars an acre.

The town was laid out and named in honor of Colonel Joseph Winston, prominent during colonial days in the councils of the patriots, and one of the heroes of the Revolution.

It became evident, day by day, that the monopoly, the community and lease systems of the Brethren would have to be abolished, which was done November 17, 1856, and the days of Moravian exclusiveness were over. The land was sold to private individuals: the Church, however, at this time owning about 1000 acres of valuable property in the Wachovia tract, much real estate in Salem rented yearly, and a bonded and loan interest approximating two hundred thousand dollars, managed still by a special church board. The Legislature of North Carolina now incorporated the town of Salem, which "took its rank with other American towns without changing in the least its ecclesiastical connections of the congregation."

The court house and jail of Winston were built in 1852, but, being isolated from railroads and no special business centreing there, its growth and improvement were slow.

The freedom from military duty granted to the Moravians at their early settlement was rescinded by an enactment of the North Carolina Legislature in 1831. During the Civil War, which devastated the country two decades and half ago, Salem and Winston sent into the Confederate service several companies of infantry, and two bands of music, which did good service, attesting upon every battle-field their courage and endurance. When the sad end came they returned to rebuild up their shattered fortunes and retrieve their losses during four years of carnage, went to work and nobly have come forth as gold tried by the fire. Politics do not disturb their calculations, party quarrels do not excite them, for while the Democrats are most numerous, many Republicans live in their midst.

The farmers of this section of country had never conceived the idea of cultivating tobacco until 1858, when three planters moved from Halifax Co., Va., and settled in the northern part of the county. They were experienced tobacco growers, and made such a success that others were stimulated to follow their example, when it soon became evident that a very superior variety of tobacco, both in flavor and quality could be raised in this and adjoining counties, and bring a better price than any other commodity. In fact, the soil, supposed poor, was found to yield rich returns of the finest "yellow leaf" tobacco, and has no superior "in texture, oil or aroma, not even in the famed leather-wood district of Henry Co., Va." Fresh lands yield from five to eight hundred pounds to the acre, old land fertilized yields about the same, but quality not quite so good. In 1870 there was not quite two hundred and fifty thousand pounds raised in the county; now, "from the best information on the subject, there are not much less than from ten to twelve million pounds used annually in the manufacture of plug tobacco alone, besides several million pounds of leaf tobacco shipped to Europe and other points." This amazing increase shows an impetus of business not excelled by any Western town in the United States.

Winston was no tobacco market until 1872, the farmers taking their produce to Danville, Va. During that year, a gentleman* came from Davie County, looking for a business location. He thought this would be a favorable point for tobacco interests and proposed opening a warehouse for the sale of leaf tobacco. There was no building better than an old frame stable to be found suitable for the purpose, but this was rented, and the sale of tobacco begun. There were at that time only about four hundred inhabitants in Winston, having been for twenty-three years only a place of small growth. The railroad connection of Richmond & Danville Road during that year afforded an outlet for trade, and factories began

* Major T. J. Brown.

to be built, until in 1875 there were five in successful operation. Since then a mighty business has grown up, millions of dollars are invested and expended yearly, twenty-nine factories for the manufacture of plug tobacco, two smoking tobacco factories, two cigar factories and twelve leaf or dry factories, have sprung up to meet the demands of the trade, and Winston, whose motto has ever since been "Excelsior," has won an enviable notoriety as a North Carolina town, known far and near through its different grades of tobacco, as a place of importance in the commercial world. Its business men, engaged in this great traffic, were mostly raised in the neighboring sections of the country, and were familiar with the growth of tobacco all their lives. Beginning operations here with small capital, they have followed up success, increased their number of workmen, discarded hand presses and the old methods, moved out of wooden buildings into commodious brick structures, and are now operating hydraulic presses run by steam pumps, with all modern improvements of drying by steam, &c., to be found any where.

Producers have learned that an acre of land will yield six or seven times as much in tobacco (from seventy-five to two hundred and fifty dollars per acre) as if grown in anything else, and no farmer is guilty of failing to follow up this great advantage, while at the same time he devotes enough space to a diversity of other crops sufficient for home consumption, thereby manifesting more wisdom than cotton growers farther South, who bulk their whole crop on the fleecy staple. Frequently as many as five hundred wagons per day make their way along the different roads of the county to the tobacco warehouses of Winston, where they receive good prices for their long and tedious labor, and return home happy with the fruit of their toil, to be expended in improved agricultural implements, the necessities and many of the luxuries of life.

## CHAPTER X.

### Cultivation of Tobacco.

From the time Sir Walter Raleigh's colonists returned to England and introduced into that country the tobacco they had found in America, it has been an article highly prized by the human family, and, although a luxury, has grown into more general use than any other substance, both sexes considering it a solace and comfort in hours of greatest disaster.

Popes and potentates thundered against its use, declaring it a crime, punishable in some countries by death. King James I. thought fit to issue against it his famous "Counterblast to Tobacco," yet steadily but surely it grew in favor with the masses, and now, after nearly three centuries have passed, it has become one of the most important articles of commerce.

Some information, therefore, with regard to its cultivation, will not be amiss, particularly to those not familiar with its growth.

The seed is sown very early in hot-beds, and transplanted, like cabbage, to hills prepared carefully in rows. This is done in damp weather. The ground is kept perfectly free from weeds by plowing and hoeing, and has to be gone over frequently to remove by hand the unsightly tobacco worms that feed upon its leaves, and would soon destroy the plants. When the flower shoot appears this has to be nipped off by hand, also all suckers removed.

Before the first frost it is cut close to the ground, with the stalk split and hung upon long sticks. These are hung upon scaffolds to dry, great care being observed that the plants are not too much crowded. There are no windows in these houses or barns, only iron or brick flues along the base, where a fire is kept continually for several days until it is cured. This makes the leaf very dry, and the planter must wait for a damp day to strip the leaves from the stalk. Then the leaves, six or eight in number, are tied together across the end, and this bundle is called "a hand of tobacco." Now it is ready for market, and in this section of the country the farmer fills the bottom of his large mountain wagon or wagons with the precious commodity, covers it with a wagon sheet, and toils along over many a weary mile, sometimes as far as sixty miles to the warehouses of Winston, where he drives in, stays all night in camp style, and then exposes his crop for sale.

A warehouse is a novel sight. It usually occupies a large space, one portion of which is reserved for the wagons and teams, sometimes as many as one hundred finding shelter beneath its roof; the other portion is where the tobacco is exposed for sale. The floor is swept very clean, the tobacco is taken from the wagons on trucks and placed in piles, with tags stuck on the end of a small stick like, so many little flags, bearing the number of pounds in each pile, the farmer's name, &c. The farmer himself classes it into different grades, regulated by color and texture, even that on the same stalk being classed differently. The most valuable is that of light color and most silky to the touch.

When the floor of the immense warehouse is covered with these piles, this is called a "break of tobacco; then the huge, clanging bell, which hangs in a cupola on the roof of the building, is rung, manufacturers and dealers hurry in, and when the crowd is collected, the auctioneer begins with his stentorian voice to halloo, and bidding by piles begins. The farmer, with anxious face and hands in pockets of his heavy overcoat, slouched hat, pants tucked into his boots, watches eagerly the progress of sale, which, if satisfactory, brings a pleased expression to his careworn brow, he whistles softly a little tune, thinks of the comforts possible for Mary and the little ones, pockets his well-earned cash, and goes back to his home happy that the crop has paid so well.

From the warehouse, the tobacco is carried to the factory on white oak baskets of peculiar shape, about four feet square, four inches deep,—as much as five to eight hundred pounds sometimes piled on a basket and hauled on drays, one basket above another until the load is complete. When received in factory, it is hung separately on racks, sometimes five deep, reaching from floor to ceiling, where it is allowed to dry thoroughly. When a damp day comes it is taken down, packed in bulk on the floor of another apartment, and remains until used, and can be kept for years in this state. From there it starts into the manufacturing process. Dealers in the leaf, after leaving warehouse, have the tobacco placed in hogsheads and ship by rail to other points. At an early day al tobacco was taken from plantation to market in hogsheds, a rude carriage of the kind constructed to haul one hogshead at a time, being one of the curiosities of the past, on exhibition at the National Museum at Washington.

# CHAPTER XI.

## How a Plug of Tobacco is Made.

The tobacco is removed from where it is placed in bulk to a large room, and put in piles on the floor. Women and men sit in chairs along the sides of this room, sometimes with stakes like a miniature fence all around their chairs, and open each leaf carefully, examine it closely, putting each kind in piles between these stakes, of the like variety. This is called "classing tobacco." Those who work at this have to be expert enough to distinghish the difference in each leaf, and be able to place it in its proper position. They seem to be well contented, as the work is light, and as their nimble fingers spread out the golden leaves, they break into songs, frequently all joining in praise to the great Father. While passing through one of these rooms we listened to the refrain, "How can I forget Him," which echoed through the vast room, and lingers in memory yet, with the picture of the busy contentment that seems to animate each worker.

From there, the tobacco is taken to the casing-room, where it is spread upon a huge platform about twenty feet square, and sprinkled with a solution of licorice and granulated sugar, with a flavoring of dried peaches, or other preferred flavor, tossed about and shaken together until perfectly distributed through the mass. After being thoroughly "cased" it is thrown through trap doors into the rolling-room below. The heat in the casing-room is very great, huge kettles holding as much as fifty gallons of the mixture, being kept boiling by steam all the time, as it must go on the tobacco warm enough to spread. The largest leaves are reserved for wrappers for the plug tobacco.

The rolling-room presents a scene not easily forgotten. Work benches from eight to ten feet in length, and two and a half or three wide, are placed in rows throughout the apartment. These benches have two sides. At one side stands the stemmers, generally two for each roller, who works on the other side of the bench. The stemmers strip the leaf from the stem, and pass over to the roller who spreads out three or four leaves together, and by a dexterous movement shapes it in form of a plug, cuts off the ragged end by a tobacco cutter, (small knife worked by lever), puts on the wrapper, weighs it on small scale which stands to the right of his bench, and then it is taken to the receiver who stands at a table on the side of the same room, where it is again weighed that each lump may be uniformly perfect.

From there it is taken and spread upon large dryers, about twelve by two feet in length. These are carried to the dry-house, where coils of steam pipes, underneath a latticed floor provides the requisite heat, about one hundred and fifty degrees Farenheit. These dryers are piled one above another until the room is filled where they remain from twelve to fifteen hours. Some of this tobacco is made in plugs, some into twists, but the process of manufacturing is identical. Plugs weigh from one to eight ounces, twist from half an ounce to seven ounces, but all packed in one box must weigh the same.

After coming from dry-house it is too brittle to handle, so is packed in large tight boxes, with lids opening from the sides where it remains until it draws sufficient moisture for "prizing."

It is then tagged by boys, who place the plugs in a tin frame and stick the tags on with brand and maker's name, sometimes tin, and sometimes paper. From there it is placed in the shapes of the presses, which look like large, upright stoves standing in rows. These shapes have twelve divisions, where the plugs are placed each separate. A sheet iron cover fits over. Twelve are arranged one above another in the steam hydraulic press, where it is subjected to a pressure of one hundred and sixty tons to the square inch. Here it remains about twenty minutes, when it is taken out by hands with small, round sticks, who strike the plugs from the shapes with wonderful rapidity. This is called "prizing tobacco."

From here it goes to another kind of press, where it is again prized in boxes. The lids are put on and the boxes are ready for the revenue stamp, which fits in a groove made in one corner. The embellishing of pictures, stamping of fancy brands, completes the job, and it is ready for shipment; but no box can leave the factory without revenue stamp, which costs eight cents per pound. These boxes weigh from ten to sixty pounds to suit the trade. The Northern market demands mostly the dark, the Southern the light tobacco.

These factories employ from two to five hundred* hands each. An elevator runs through the buildings, each floor is provided with Fairbank's scales, speaking tubes and telephone. The temperature of working rooms must never be lower than eighty degrees steam heat. The tobacco stems are piled in bundles in the upper floor of factory and shipped to Europe, where they are made into snuff and a low grade of smoking tobacco.

The negro is in his element in a tabacco factory, preferring to work in crowds. Here he works and breaks forth into songs; those in the rolling and prize rooms particular to greet visitors with some swelling, echoing chorus they consider a choice entertainment.

The rollers employ their own stemmers, and the factory owners make their contracts with them. Payment is made every two weeks, and it is estimated from sixty to seventy-five thousand dollars per month is thus paid out, and goes into other branches of trade, making the tobacco interests of Winston one of prime importance to every class of business.

## CHAPTER XII.

### The Churches.

The Methodist Protestant church membership was moved from Liberty to Winston in 1850, to a frame house upon the site of the present brick building, which was erected at a cost of three thousand five hundred dollars. There are two hundred and ten communicants. The pastor is Rev. W. A. Swaim, native of Washington County, N. C., and a graduate of Yadkin College, N. C.

The Methodist Episcopal church South organization was moved from Jerusalem, about a mile north of the city, to Winston in 1852. A small brick building was erected on the site of the present commodious edifice, and used as a house of worship until four years ago, when the Centenary M. E. church was built, at a cost of twenty-seven thousand dollars. It is one of the most elegant churches in the South,—the main auditorium with a seating capaity of one thousand, and the annex, which opens out direct from

* P. H. Hanes & Co.

M. E. Church, Winston, N. C.

the pulpit, with sliding doors, seating five hundred, used as Sabbath School room, for social church meetings, but thrown into one large audience room when the crowd is great by simply opening the immense sliding doors. The building is supplied with water, heated by a furnace in basement, and lighted by gas-jets, arranged around a circular concave surface in ceiling. The architecture is in the graceful modern style, with tower rising from one side. The windows are gothic style, stained glass, two of which are memorials of faithful servants gone home to rest. There are broad galleries three sides of the building; in the back gallery is a large pipe organ, recently put up at a cost of thirty-five hundred dollars, of exquisite tone. The membership numbers over six hundred. Rev. W. F. Norman, a native of Davidson County and graduate of Trinity College, is the pastor.

The Presbyterian church of Winston was organized in 1862, and a temporary house of worship built. Last year twelve thousand dollars was raised, and a handsome, commodious edifice, with tower and spire, occupies the old site on Cherry Street, and will soon be dedicated. Will have stained glass windows, all the modern improvements of heating and lighting, and a small pipe organ, already in position. This church, standing at the intersection of one of the streets leading from the public square, is an ornament to the place. Rev. E. P. Davis, graduate of Davidson College, N. C., and Theological Seminary of S. C., is pastor.

The Baptists were organized in 1871, and five years later their present church was built, costing four thousand dollars, with some later improvements. Church membership two hundred and thirty-five. Rev. H. A. Brown, graduate of Wake Forest College, N. C., is pastor.

The Baptists and Methodists have each a chapel in different localities of town.

The Episcopal church was organized, with two members, in 1877. Shortly afterwards the church was built at a cost of three thousand dollars. The congregation had a most efficient rector from Brooklyn, N. Y., last year, but he died very suddenly in Washington, and the pulpit has not been supplied. Rev. Mr. Lacy did a good work for the denomination, was a true man, but ill-health compelled him to relinquish his charge.

The Moravian church has already been described. Besides this, known as "the Home church," there are Elm Street, East Salem and Colored churches in Salem, no other denomination but

Moravian in the town, and also a chapel in Winston, on what is known as the Reservation, a tract still held by Moravians. They have a membership of over a thousand. Rev. Edward Rondthaler, of Pennsylvania, graduate of Theological Seminary, Bethlehem, Pa., and of schools in Europe, is pastor. The degree of D. D. was conferred on him by University at Chapel Hill, N. C. Rev. John McCuiston is his assistant, holding the several chapel services, and otherwise aiding in the work of the ministry. He is a native of Forsyth County, a theological student of Dr. Rondthaler, devoted to a life-work of Christian usefulness.

---

## CHAPTER XIII.

### Various Interests.

Winston-Salem have each a well-equipped Fire Department, that of Salem dating back more than a hundred years, when the the first fire engine in America was brought for their use from Germany.

The Masons, Knights Templar, Knights and Ladies of Honor, and Odd Fellows have lodges in working order in both towns.

The First National Bank, the Wachovia National, and the Five Cent Savings Bank, have their stockholders in both cities, but the banks have their places of business in Winston, with an assured capital of several hundred thousand dollars, "regularly declaring 8 and 10 per cent. dividends, and stand solid in all respects."

Winston has a fine graded school building, the outcome of the efforts of her citizens in 1877 towards free-school education—costing twenty-five thousand dollars including furniture, planned by Colonel J. W. Alspaugh, Secretary of the Board of Education, "It is a two-story brick in T form, having a length of 190 feet and a depth, including Chapel or Assembly room of 170 feet. The imposing tower runs up four stories and with belfry and spire attains a height of 112 feet. It has nine school rooms, ample halls, a large assembly room, a commodious library and office, all elegantly fitted up. The library is worthy of special mention, as it contains a most extensive outlay of pedagogic and other works which are a great auxiliary to both teachers and pupils, amounting to the aggregate of over $4,000 worth of books. Altogether, both inside and out, the building is handsomely designed and equipped, and may be called "the crowning glory of Winston." Number of pupils in attendance, 533.

The Colored Graded School is a two-story frame structure in the eastern part of the city, and cost, including grounds and furniture, $8,500, and contains eight rooms. It has a corps of colored teachers, with one thousand children in attendance.

Both schools are managed by a Board of Education: Maj. W. A. Whitaker, *Chairman;* Col. J. W. Alspaugh, *Secretary;* Messrs. Jas. A. Gray, M. W. Norfleet, R. W. Brown.

They are under the superintendece of Prof. W. A. Blair, of High Point, N. C., graduate of Haverford College, Pa., degree of A. B., graduate of Harvard University, degree A. B., graduate of Johns Hopkins University, Baltimore. He is also editor of *The Schoolteacher*, an aducational journal, published in Winston.

He is ably assisted by three gentlemen and six lady teachers. This is considered one of the finest public schools in the State.

The Public School in Salem has not, as yet, assumed a graded form, which it is expected to do during this year, as a lot has been purchased and plans made for a brick building. The attendance is one hundred and fifty. Mr. S. A. Hege, of Salem, is Principal, with one male assistant. There are, perhaps, as many as half dozen private, primary schools in Salem; Boys' Male Academy, under charge of Moravian Church since 1791, and Female Academy, which accounts for the want of interest in public education.

In 1827 was begun the publishing of *The Farmers' and Planters' Almanac* in Salem, which has been a continuous annual publication by the same family ever since. The calculations have been made according to the German style of calendars, and have always been considered accurate and reliable, the circulation more extended through the Southern States than any publication in North Carolina. The Salem Printing Office, by J. C. Blum, proprietor of the Almanatc, was established in 1827, when the first newspaper in North Carolina was published, *The Weekly Gleaner*. The office is still in operation, using now steam presses. The name of paper issued weekly has changed several times, but known as *The People's Press* since 1851. The business is still carried on by L. V. & E. T. Blum, sons of the first proprietor.

*The Sentinel*, of Winston, was established in 1856 by some of its enterprising citizens. The present editar, Mr. Vernon Long, is a graduate of Chapel Hill, N. C. It is a weekly, full of interesting matter.

*The Union Republican*, of Winston, established in 1872, has been a successful weekly paper under the management of J. W. Goslen, a native of the county, and graduate of Trinity College. Being run in the interest of the Republican party, it has been ever dignified in its course and entirely just towards the opposite party.

*The Twin-City Daily* has been published in Winston, as an evening paper, for five years; since 1886 under the editorship of Mr. J. O. Foy. It is bright and newsy, devoted to the best interests of the people of Winston-Salem, and has a large circulation.

The Twin-City Club is an organization of the *elite* of both places, with over one hundred male members, occupying apartments in the upper part of the Gray block. The institution is governed by high moral sentiment and no gambling, betting, &c., is allowed. They have a good library, billiard room, and other comforts for the use of members, and a dance hall where their balls are given. S. E. Allen, *President;* R. L. Crawford, *Secretary*.

The Reform Club also have their rooms in Winston.

The Young Men's Christian Association, organized only one year ago, by young men of both towns, but have expended over seventoen hundred dollars in furniture, gymnasium and books, with a comfortable reading-room in Winston, where first-class newspapers and periodicals are always to be found, inviting the stranger at all times to a hearty welcome. Prof. W. A. Blair, *President;* E. L. Harris, *General Secretary;* W. B. Pollard, *Treasurer.*

The Philharmonic Society, of Salem, is composed of musical members from both cities, ladies and gentlemen of fine culture. E. A. Ebert, *President;* G. H. Rights, *Secretary;* A. N. Atwater, *Treasurer.*

The Salem Orchestra is considered one of the finest in the South, its members strictly moral and refined. They are supplied with stringed instruments, violins, cornets, flutes and horns, of the best manufacture. W. Peterson, *Leader;* B. J. Pfohl, *Secretary and Treasurer.*

Both these organizations are under the direction of Professor George Markgraff, Musical Director of Salem Female Academy. They meet weekly at the Music Hall, Salem, in the Museum building. Their concerts, given generally for benevolent purposes, are well attended, and considered rare treats by the appreciative.

The Salem Brass Band is popular through all the surrounding country, under the leadership of Prof. D. T. Crouse, who was leader of a band in the Confederate army.

The Museum, in Salem, has some rare curiosities, collected by the Young Men's Missionary Society of the Moravian Church, organized about fifty years ago Many of the contributions have been donated by foreign missionaries, while others are relics of early Moravian times. Large glass show cases, filled with the minerals of the country, petrifactions and precious stones, and many from all over the world, are ranged along the walls; cases of shells, every known variety; large collections of butterflies; reptiles in alcohol; stuffed birds; anaconda; alligator, crocodile; sea turtle; musk deer, &c.; varieties of woods; varieties of bird's eggs, including the ostrich; specimens of coral; sea-weed; Indian relics; military weapons of Revolutionary and Confederate times, are here found. There is a large number of old books: amongst them a German Bible, leather back and brass bound, printed in 1569. A cream-colored, glazed, tile stove, decorated with leaves, six feet high, with claw legs, stands on one side of the principal room, as there are two large apartments in this building. The first piano brought to Salem occupies a prominent position, once belonging to the Salem hotel, and was used during General Washington's visit for his entertainment, An odd instrument for taking profiles, before the days of Daguerre; a wooden foot stove, with heater, used in travelling; small loom for weaving tape for domestic use by the ladies; reels of different kinds; flax wheels, where was spun the beautiful linen kept as heirlooms in the families of Salem; German travelling baskets, used by first settlers; old clock from Sister's House; leather buckets of the first fire engine; stamps for printing calico; bottles and pitchers of China- and glass-ware; ship trunks; first street lamp used in Salem, 1789; parchment covered Bibles; high-backed chairs, similar to the one donated by the Brethren to the North Carolina Room at Mt. Vernon, and many other things are seen in the general collection. There is an Esquimo case; a Chinese corner, with idol, lacquered ware, tea chests, and all kinds of their work; a large collection of valuable coins from all countries, and a beautiful exhibit of Colonial and Continental State and United States currency. One of these is amusing:

*TWO PENCE.*

*We, or either of us, promise to pay Two Pence on demand.*

*Salem, Oct. 22, 1803.*

*CONRAD KRAISER.*

This was a check for change in a store. One collection is of especial interest, the travelling outfit of the Moravians who came from Pennsylvania and settled at Bethabara, consisting of a small iron pot, pewter plates and cups, tea-pot, coffee-pot, gallon, quart, pint and gill measures, lard-oil lamp, all made of the same metal, and occupying a corner alone. Above is ranged specimens of the early pottery,— the large dish which was the old pottery sign, decorated in colors, brown, green and yellow, 1773, being most prominent; then specimens of tableware, ornaments for mantels, moulds for pewter plates, as everything practical and ornamental was made at that pottery that could be moulded in clay. Around the room are framed certificates of the skill of their early workmen brought from Europe, as, according to the old custom, no man was allowed to ply his trade without such a certificate, oil paintings donated by citizens brought over with their household treasures; some of them said to have been done by some of the old masters, at any rate they are very fine. There is a steel print of Count Zinzendorf and his wife, Erdmuth Dorothea; steel engravings of Amos Comenius, done before his death, in 1670; Christian David, and others, whose names have been mentioned in sketch of Moravians; noted Bishops and brethren, amongst them that of Peter Boehler, the devoted Moravian in whose company John Wesley, founder of the Methodists, crossed the ocean during his voyage to America, and to whom he declared he owed his conversion. The high pulpit, with sounding board above, brass candlesticks and chandeliers used in the Salem church when first built, in 1800, are preserved here intact, and many, many things we have not the space to mention. Altogether it is a great pleasure and education to visit the museum, and relic hunters would think they were singularly blessed to take a peep within its walls. Visitors are expected to drop a mite in the contribution box to assist in keeping the collections in order. A portion of these things was taken to the State Exposition at Raleigh in 1884, with the exhibit of fancy-work and art from the Academy during the eighty years of its establishment, together with the county exhibit carefully collected, and Forsyth gained the one hundred dollar premium offered for the finest county exhibit in North Carolina. The money was donated to the Oxford Masonic Orphan Asylum, and Forsyth has the honor of being the banner county of the State.

The oldest house of Salem is a large log cabin, one and a half story—in continuation of the old pottery—which was established in 1772 by Gottfried Aust, on another site. All kinds of articles for domestic use, tiles for covering houses, tile stoves, and many ornamental articles were once manufactured here. The present proprietor devotes himself exclusively to the making of clay pipes, as there is another pottery where flower pots, crocks and jars are made. The clay used for the purpose is the white clay, which is first ground in a mud mill, then dampened and pounded on a large block with a mallet until it becomes the consistency of dough. It is then rolled by hand on a long table, until it stretches over a yard in length, about an inch in thickness, and is then cut in lengths of three inches. These are placed, one at a time, in a tin pipe mould, which is inclosed in a kind of small press or machine which works with a lever by hand, a hole is made through the small end by an awl and the pipe is made. They are turned out in rows on dryers where they remain several days, when they are trimmed off with a pen-knife by hand and packed in earthen-ware cases called "sagers." These are packed in a kiln and burned one day, when they are ready for market. Fifteen hundred are made per day and shipped north as far as Baltimore and Philadelphia, as far south as mobile, Ala. Salem clay pipes have quite a reputation. "Made from strong and porous clay they are distinct in themselves. By virtue of their porosity they absorb nicotine freely, and when foul from use may be burned clear in any ordinary fire."

M. P. Church, Winston, N. C.

## CHAPTER XIV.

### Associations of Ladies and Children.

The Twin-City Hospital in Winston is the result of the united efforts of the ladies of both places, suggested by Mr. Lacy,—late minister of the Episcopal church—and has been in operation since December, 1887. The Commissioners of the two towns pay rent for the house, and physicians give their services. There is a membership of one hundred and eighty-eight members who pay weekly dues. Money is raised also by concerts, lectures, suppers. A visiting committee of two ladies for each week is appointed at each monthly meeting, who attend to wants of the matron who manages the establishment. Expenses since opening, $1,271.49.

Officers—Mrs. J. M. Rogers, President ; Mrs. A. B. Gorrell, Secretary ; Mrs. E. E. Shelton, Treasurer.

The Benevolent Society, composed of members of all churches, has been organized two years, to aid the worthy poor, confined to the limits of Winston. A committee from each ward is appointed to look after the indigent in their several districts. Each member pays yearly dues, and the purses of the citizens are ever open to the managers, who collect by subscriptions, and all applications for charity are referred to this Society.

Mrs. C. H. Wiley, President ; Mrs. M. Prather, Secretary ; Mrs. J. W. Alspaugh, Treasurer.

The Ladies' Auxiliary of the Y. M. C. A. was formed in Jan., 1889 with membership of seventy ladies from both places. They have furnished the parlor of the Association, and expended three hundred dollars money, and presents given, entertained the District Association, and given several dinners and entertainments to the gentlemen.

Mrs. Bitting, President ; Mrs. M. Williamson, Treasurer ; Mrs. Henry Fries, Cor. Sec. ; Mrs. J. M. Rogers, Rec. Secretary.

The Womens' Christian Temperance Union was organized February, 1884. Members are required to sign the Temperance pledge. "Different subjects are discussed at each weekly meeting; as its object is the uplifting of humanity." There are forty-two members. They have raised and expended in the different departments of their work five hundred dollars.

Mrs. J. P. Ector, President.

The Female Missionary Society of Baptist church, Winston has been in working order twelve years. Dues are collected regularly and funds sent through the church to Association. They raised last year for foreign missions fifty-five dollars.

Mrs. H. A. Brown, President and Treasurer.

Ladies' Aid Society of Baptist church organized March, 1886, its object being to assist the church where most needed. $551.84 has been raised by various suppers, &c. Members twenty-five.

Mrs. Dr. Watkins, President; Mrs. E. O. Allen, Treasurer; Miss Fannie Cox, Secretary.

The Sunbeam Society of Children of Baptist church has sixty-seven members. Its object is to study the manners and customs of different countries towards missionary efforts. Since March, '89, they have raished $71.00 to assist with State missionary work.

Ladies' Parish Aid Society of Episcopal church organized March 22, 1886, with rector as President, and lady Vice-Presidents. Amount raised to date, $159.00.

Mission Society, Presbyterian church, devoted to foreign missions exclusively—organized 1875. Has thirty members. Amount contributed to present time, $697.60.

Mrs. H. D. Lott, President; Mrs. R. Glenn, Secretary; Mrs. J. B. Watkins, Treasurer.

Ladies' Aid Society, of Presbyterian church, organized 1885. Their object was to assist in raising funds for building their new church. With forty members they succeeded in paying over $1400.00 to the building committee.

Mrs. Sophy Lanier, President; Miss Watkins, Secretary; Mrs. H. D. Lott, Treasurer.

The Happy Sailors with Christ as their Captain, is a Society of boys in the Presbyterian church. Has twelve paying members—been in operation three years. They made a Christmas offering to the Thornwell Orphan Asylum at Clinton, S. C., and have paid for pulpit of new church.

Mrs. E. J. Lott, Matron.

Methodist Protestant Ladies' Aid Society, organized 1888—devoted to lending assistance to any branch of church work. It has supplied the church with new carpets, chandeliers, Bible and stove, and assisted with pastor's salary, expending $187.00. Membership 30.

Mrs. S. Starr, President; Mrs. B. F. Norman, Sec. and Treas.

Womens' Missionary Society of Methodist Episcopal Church South, organized 1879. Has raised and expended $931.79.

Mrs. R. S. Davis, President; Mrs. Frank Martin, Secretary; Mrs. Celeste Alspaugh, Treasurer.

Bright Jewels Juvenile Methodist E. Church Society. Auxiliary to Womens' Missionary Society, organized 1886. Has fifty-seven members. Money raised $157.90.

Mrs. M. L. Hendren, Lady Manager: Miss Gertie Vaughn, President: Miss Katie Hanes, Recording Sec.: Miss Mamie Gray, Treasurer.

The Salem Female Missionary Society, organized 1822—in aid of the mission to the colored people of Salem and vicinity. A church was built for their use and a missionary appointed to preach for them. This mission was supported thirty-six years, when it was placed in charge of Salem Congregation, where it still remains. They have also made donations to foreign missions having raised $4,587.74, and are still devoting their energies to the work of missions.

Dr. E. Rondthaler, President; Mrs E. Rondthaler, Treasurer; Miss A. Steiner, Secretary.

The Salem Home for aged and infirm women and orphan children, is a well-conducted establishment under the guidance of the "King's Daughters," who work in bands of ten. The first ten are directors, another ten supplies clothing, another provisions, another fuel, &c. This is a regular incorporated institution, owned by a board of trustees, with executive committee of ten. A building was purchased and paid for costing two thousand dollars. They afford relief and a home for thirty occupants with a matron in charge, everything managed in systematic, substantial manner. There are ten or tweve bands.

Mrs. F. Fries, President Board of Trustees ; Mrs. E. W. Lineback, Chairman Executive Committee.

## CHAPTER XV.

This little pamphlet we send forth to the people is as near correct as possible to be made. We have consulted the best authorities on all historical points, and have culled much useful information from the newspapers published in Winston-Salem. We have also compared all this with the traditions amongst the oldest inhabitants, visited in person the warehouses and tobacco factories and then read our articles on those subjects to our advertisers who are engaged in that business—so the estimates of trade in this particular branch of industry might not be considered exaggerated.

---

To Prof. Blair, Superintendent of the Winston Graded School, we are indebted for correct information on the educational subject.

---

We are under obligations to Miss Elizabeth March, of the Winston Graded School, for collecting from their secretaries the report of organization and money expended by the ladies' and children's church and charitable societies of Winston, and to Miss Steiner and Mrs. E. A. Ebert, for those of Salem.

---

We were kindly shown through the Salem Museum by Mr. J. A. Linebach, who has taken much interest and devoted many years in gathering together and arranging for the Young Men's Missionary Society, now extinct, the very valuable collection, which is one of the finest to be found anywhere.

---

"Sunset on Pilot Mountain," a gem from the pen of Miss E. A. Lehman, at the head ot Literary Department of Salem Female

Academy, many years, and also editor of *Academy*, we are sure will be appreciated by our readers. In point of intellectuality Miss Lehman is the peer of any woman in the South.

---

The touching little story, "The Guardian Angel," is a true incident in the history of Bethabara, given us by a literary gentleman of Salem.

---

"How Oft I've Trod that Shadowy Way," we have been granted permission to use by the author John Henry Boner—a native of Salem whose name has become familier In the leading periodicals of the day. His work, "Whispering Pines," published several years ago, entitled him to rank as one of North Carolina's leading poets. He is at present connected with *The Century* Magazine, New York.

---

Such are the facts, incidents and histories of the Twin-Cities of North Carolina—which we have faithfully sought to chronicle. We have endeavored to show the character of the early pioneers whose settlements stretched in a continuous line along the entire Wachovia tract. We have also tried to show that the immense business interests of Winston-Salem is not the result of capital from abroad but the outcome of individual enterprise and energy of her native born citizens who have developed their own resources in a remarkable manner. Last, but not least, the people themselves are possessed of the highest tone of moral character. Cherishing reverently the traditions of their forefathers, emulating all that was good in their institutions, going forward in the line of duty—improving upon the solid foundation of the past they form a society that has no superior within the broad bounds of the United States. To set this in a true light that others may catch the reflection, has been to us a labor intensely interesting.

Gray Block, Winston, N. C.

# CHAPTER XVI.

## OUR ADVERTISERS.

### F. & H. Fries.

In the year 1840 Mr. Francis Fries, who had previously been Superintendent of the Salem Cotton Manufacturing Co., established for himself a small wool carding establishment. As his business increased he added new machines, and in 1846 still further enlarged his mill and associated with him his brother, Mr. H. W. Fries, who is the Senior member of the present firm.

Under the name F. & H. Fries the business increased rapidly, and in addition to wool carding, spinning and weaving, a cotton mill was started in 1848, the building being erected by the side of their woolen mill.

In 1859 they established gas works, which are still in active operation, and supply gas to the Female Academy, Salem church and many private dwellings.

Upon the death of Mr. Francis Fries in 1863, the business was conducted by Mr. H. W. Fries, and from that date until 1879 several additions were made in their buildings.

During that year the firm was re-organized and while the original firm name of F. & H. Fries was retained, the members of the firm were increased so that at present is composed of Messrs. H. W. Fries, J. W. Fries, F. H. Fries and H. E. Fries.

In 1880 and 1881 the new firm erected a large cotton factory called the "Arista Mill" separate and apart from the woolen mill. The quality of goods manufactured has made for the firm and mill such a reputation they are not able to fill the numerous orders from all sections of the country.

During the present year the firm have enlarged "Wachovia Flouring Mills," which they have been running since 1877, and now have an elevator built after the most modern ideas, with a capacity of 30,000 bushels of grain, while their mills grind daily, at least a car load of grain.

All the various mills of F. & H. Fries are supplied with modern machinery and conveniences. They were among the first, if not the first, to introduce electric lights into their mills, while in addition to the water works of the town, they have their own fire-pumps, and have their mills thickly covered with water pipes and automatic sprinklers.

All these mills are run by engines bought of Messrs. Robert Wetherill & Co., Chester, Penn.

The members of firm are all engaged in public enterprises. Mr. H. W. Fries has been for years Director of the N. C. R. R. Co. Mr. J. W. Fries is Trustee of State University, Salem Female Academy, Director of the N. W. N. C. R. R. Co., and one of the Board of County Commissioners. Mr. F. H. Fries is President of the Va. & N. C. Construction Co., and has in complete and running condition 30 miles of the Roanoke & Southern Railway. Mr. H. E. Fries is Trustee of the A. & M. College at Raleigh, also of Davidson College, and is at present Mayor of Salem.

FRIES, GIERSH & SENSEMAN, *General Merchandise.*

One of the largest mercantile houses in Salem is that mentioned above. H. W. Fries the senior partner is well known in manufacturing, H. A. Giersh is a native of Salem, six years a merchant and in '87 became a partner as above. Mr. Senseman is in the stove trade as noticed elsewhere. The firm keeps a full line of general merchandise and does a leading trade. They also keep a full line of Ziegler Brother's popular manufacture of fine shoes, for men, women and children's wear, and the sales for the past twelve months show a large advance over previous years. Fries, Giersh & Senseman have a considerable jobbing trade but give special attention to their large retail business, occupying three stories with their wares, and are the leading house in Salem merchandise.

W. O. SENSEMAN & CO., *Stoves, Tin and Sheet Iron Merchandise.*

Has been conducted at the sign of the big coffee pot, in Salem, for thirty-three years, first J. E. Mickey, then G. A. Boozer, Giersh, Senseman & Co. (H. E. Fries). Since January, 1885, W. O. Senseman & Co. (H. E. Fries). Tobacco flues are one of their specialties and tinware, at wholesale and retail, with grates, heaters, cooking stoves. All the members of the firm are natives of Salem.

A C. VOGLER & SON, SALEM, N. C., *Undertaking and Furniture*

A C Vogler is a native of Salem, and after a five year's apprenticeship with the venerable John D. Siewers, he opened up a cabinet shop on his present site, thirty years ago Mr Vogler added ready-made goods to meet modern progression, now has a good assortment of furniture, ordering the finer grades by sample, when desired. This house manufactures common coffins and furnishes fine caskets to meet his demand in undertaking. In this line his trade spreads out over a wide territory, and with a quarter of a century's experience, every requisite to the last sad rides is carefully looked after. With January, '87, Mr. V. admitted his son, Frank H., as a partner. Frank has since received a diploma from the Oriental School of Embalmers, and is secretary of the North Carolina Undertaker's Association. The trade of the firm extends out for a radius of twenty miles or more.

F. C. MEINUNG.

The above named gentleman is actively engaged in the manufacturing and repairing of carriages, wagons and trucks, and occupies the old stand of his father on Main street, Salem. The business was established in 1837 by Mr. H. E. Meinung, father of Mr. F. C. Meinung the present proprietor who in 1884 succeeded his father in business. He has had many years experience having learned the trade quite young. His shop is well provided with all the modern mechanical appliances necessary in the business, and he gives constant employment to a number of skilled workmen. None but the best materials are used in the construction of his work. Mr. Meinung pays close attention to his duties, personally superintending all work done, and never failing in giving perfect satisfaction.

ASHCRAFT & OWENS, WINSTON,

occopy store in the Gray Block fronting on two streets, a large elegant store sufficient with everything in the Drug line, and do a thriving business. Mr. Bertram Owens is a native of Birmingham, Pa., and graduated at Nassau National College of Pharmacy. Mr. Henry Ashcraft, native of Monroe, N. C., where he conducted a successful business several years. They are enterprising young men. Commenced operations in Winston, February, 1886.

## ROSENBACHER BROTHERS, WINSTON, N. C.,
*Dry Goods, Clothing and Furnishing.*

The separation of different lines of trade is an enterprise that enables a firm to carry a larger and more complete assortment in a special branch and give closer attention to its details, and the above firm has done its share towards the division of the various lines of trade in this city. Three separate stores are conducted by this house The clothing and gents' furnishing house occupies the double front Buxton building 40x85 feet and is said to be the largest room and best assortment of clothing to be found in the State of North Carolina, comprising all sizes and qualities demanded in the trade. Two rooms of the fine Gray block, 25x85 each, and communicating by an archway, are filled with a complete assortment in their lines. One department comprises dry goods, carpets and millinery, the other is devoted to hats and shoes exclusively. The shoe store is thoroughly filled with everything desirable in foot wear. We cannot go into the minutia of this extensive concern, but will simply say that Rosenbacher Bros. are shrewd buyers, are fully alive to the interests of their customers and there is nothing that a lady could desire in dry goods, domestics or notions but what they endeavor to keep. A dozen clerks find employment in these three stores and a large business is transacted. The partners are of German nativity and in trade at Arcola four years prior to engaging in the trade of this place in 1880.

Phillip Christopher Vogler, the ancestor of all the Voglers in North Carolina, was born in 1725 in the Palatinate on the Rhine. He first emigrated to Broadbay, Me., and from thence to this vicinity in 1770.

John Vogler, his grandson, who lived to the advanced age of 97 years, commenced the watchmakers trade about 1800, and was succeeded by his son E. A. Vogler, with whom W. T. Vogler was associated until 1871, when he set up in business for himself.

In 1879 Mr Vogler becoming convinced that Winston would be the centre of trade, removed his store here, but continuing to reside in Salem.

The location is on Main St., opposite the Merchants' Hotel, and as the establishment, from its commencement, has enjoyed the patronage of our best citizens, Mr. Vogler has been enabled to fit up his store very handsomely, and displays a large stock in every department of the jewelry trade.

His son Henry E. Vogler, has recently taken a thorough course in Optics, in New York, and is now successfully fitting glasses to persons who have defective visions.

S. E. ALLEN, *Dealer in Hardware, China, Crockery, &c.*, moved from Raleigh, N. C. to Winston in 1876. He was raised in Granville county, connected with Richmond & Danville Railroad as general ticket and passenger agent before moving to Raleigh. Mr. Allen is a citizen alive to all the interests of progression, a safe reliable gentleman of strict moral character.

H. W. SHORE, *Groceries and Confectionery.*

H. W. Shore was born in this vicinity and has lived in Salem over 35 years. He was for a long time a clerk in the post-office and served for thirteen years as postmaster. In Dec. '82 he opened his stock of merchandise at the corner of Main and New Shallow-ford Sts., where he keeps a full line of family and fancy groceries, queensware, confectioneries and cigars. Mr. Shore has a large acquaintance throughout the country.

BROWN & BROWN, WINSTON, N. C.

*Druggists and Opera House Lessees.*

Smith & Brown fitted up the commodious drug rooms near the corner Fourth and Liberty streets in 1882 and a year since F. C. Brown purchased the interest of Maj. Smith making the firm name Brown & Brown. The Browns are both natives of Davie county, N. C., having come to Winston in 1872, and in 1880 engaged with Maj. Smith in the drug enterprise. F. C. Brown has long been principal salesman with W. T. Carter & Co. The store is finely fitted up having handsome shelf ware, soda fountain, etc. The management is in the hands of W. C. Brown whose long service in business leaves it unnecessary for us to add further comment. This firm also has the management of Brown's Opera House.

W. P. ORMSBY, SALEM, N. C.,

*Dealer in Pianos, Organs and Musical Merchandise and Agent for Domestic Sewing Machines,*

is a native of England. Has been in the business ten years having had branch stores in Winston, Salem and Greensboro. Was the first to open a music store in the Twin-Cities. He is a practical musician playing first violin in the Salem Orchestra. Mr. Ormsby worked for years in a piano manufactory in Europe and is an ingenious artist in wood. He has made a ladies folding desk which is a rare piece of workmanship using eight thousand eight hundred pieces of wood, thirty five covering space of a silver dime. In its construction he employed thirty-five varieties of wood imported from China, Persia, Africa, Australia, Brazil, Italy, France and England. It is artistically inlaid in stars, flowers, musical instruments and fruits. The desk is eighteen inches long, ten wide when unfolded, five inches deep, with five tiny secret drawers. He spent ten years in arranging it as desired, and values it at fifteen hundred dollars. He has taken premiums at State Exposition, and will send it to the Columbus Centennial where it will no doubt be accorded first premium for the most remarkable piece of mechanical skill. His business is in a flourishing condition, as he is ever ready to attend to orders.

### Dr. J. F. Shaffner

is engaged in the drug business Salem—a native of the place His father, a native of Switzerland came to Salem in 1834. His brother had emigrated in 1818. The old gentleman was fond of relating his first experience in America. As he was coming on stage from Fredericksburg to Richmond en route to Salem, they were overtaken by the meteoric shower or falling of the stars, people are so fond of relating. Thinking it one of the peculiarities of a new country, he was not alarmed until the stage-driver unhitched his horses and refused to proceed until the strange phenomenon was over. Dr. Shaffner is an energetic business man, owning also a bone mill where bones are crushed and sold as a fertilizer to the farmers in surrounding country. He has also, a cotton gin, but gins only about one hundred bales per year, as that article is not much raised by farmers in this vicinity. His son, Mr. Henry Shaffner, is proprietor of Salem clay pipe factory.

### The First National Bank of Winston

was organized March, 1876, with a capital of $50,000, which was shortly afterwards increased to $100,000. The bank has a present surplus and undivided profits of $65,000, has regularly declared 10 per cent. dividends and stands solid in all respects.

J. A. Bitting, a native of Stokes County, was elected as President of the institution upon its opening, and shortly after removed to Winston, where he has assisted in developing manufacturing and other progressive matters of the city. J. W. Alspaugh is a native of this place, was a practicing attorney and negotiated loans for the capitalists of this vicinity prior to commencing the banking business as cashier of the First National on its opening in 1876. Col. Alspaugh was Mayor at different times, for several years editor and proprietor of the *Sentinel*, and has been more or less identified with every movement for the public good.

### Racket Store, *Winston.*

D. D. Schouler, proprietor, was brought up in the mercantile trade of New York city, and six years ago located in this place. He keeps a large line of Dry Goods, Millinery, Fancy Goods, Notions and stationery next door to the Post Office, a few months since on account of his extensive ladies' trade having removed the Gents' Furnishing, Clothing and Goods in that line to a store-room across the street in the Liberty Block, where auction sales are conducted every night. The Dry Goods house is furnished with the elevated cash system, the counter-sunk, unique show-case plan, and is conveniently arranged throughout. Mr. Schouler is well satisfied with his success in Winston, and has invested in real estate and building to the improvement of the place.

### B. F. Hanes, *Manufacturer of Plug, Twist and Fancy Tobaccos.*

This plant was established by Mr. Hanes in 1886, who started business without a brand or a customer. By steady perseverance, sound judgment, indomitable pluck, coupled with fair dealing, and the manufacture of honest goods, his success has been almost phenomenal.

His tobacco works are not only a model of their kind; a monument to the man and an ornament to the city and the trade, but among the most extensive in the South.

Now, in 1889, the fourth year of the business, the output in net work in the boxes is six hundred thousand pounds.

Mr. Hanes is himself a practical manufacturer, acquainted with the details in every department, from the warehouse floors where the leaf is purchased, to the storage rooms of the factory, where the long rows of boxes containing the manufactured goods, displays the several brands to charming advantage. He not only gives a personal supervision to every department in his large establishment but makes his own selection of the stock and material used in the manufacture of every one of his justly celebrated and popular brands, whether common or fancy stock. Hence his goods have steadily climbed up into popular favor and to-day stand as first class favorites. Mr. Hanes does an extensive business and is well and favorably known as a tobacco manufacturer throughout North Carolina, South Carolina, Georgia, Alabama, Mississippi, Tennessee, Florida, Texas, Virginia and West Virginia.

His goods and brands are well known and appreciated; an evidence of the fact is the large and increasing demand in Baltimore, Philadelphia and Washington City. The goods of B. F. Hanes have found their way to the golden doors of California and of New Mexico. There, in a far away land of strangers to all North Carolina tobacco, they have found friends and are constantly duplicating themselves. All he asks is a trial."

EBERT, PAYNE & CO., *Tobacco Manufacturers, Winston,* have been associated together only one year. Mr. E. A. Ebert is a native of Salem, his father one of the early Moravian settlers. He was interested in the tobacco business with W. W. Wood & Co. until their dissolution, when the present firm was established. Mr. R. M. Payne moved from Davie County in 1885, has his residence in Winston, while his partner resides in Salem. They have done a successful business during this year, their tobacco is becoming known on the market, and they have an encouraging outlook for the future. Mr. Ebert is a prominent Mason and Knight Templar, and President several years of the Salem Phillharmonic Society.

THE BELO HOUSE, *Salem,*

is occupied by Mrs. J. A. Hansly as a boarding-house for the accommodation of families and travelling men, who find there first-class fare and good attention. Mrs. Hanby is a native of Wilmington, N. C., kept hotel at Wilson several years, and subsequently at Kinston, from whence she moved to Salem last summer. She rented the old family mansion of the Belos, and is seeking to make it a pleasant stopping place for patrons of the Female Academy, being only two blocks distant from that institution. The place was handsomely improved by the elder Mr. Belo, whose father settled the lot, reached by flights of stone steps from the street. At the top of each reposes successively an iron fawn, greyhound and lion. Iron railings along a stone wall, high up above the street, encircle a tastily laid off flower garden, with large conservatory to the right.

The Virginia creeper covers one end of the large building in a mass of living green, while a graceful iron veranda extends across the entire front of the house. No lovelier place could be selected as a boarding place, either permanently or temporarily, while Mrs. Hansly is a lady who understands making her guests feel perfectly at home beneath her roof.

BROWN, ROGERS & CO., *Winston*,

do a thriving hardware business in a double front store under Brown's Opera House. The building is 90 feet deep, and the outlay in all kinds of hardware is complete. They also make a specialty of Agricultural Implements, Steam Engines, Mill Supplies, and keep on hand a large stock of Buggies and all kinds of Carriage Material, with regard to the special wants of the farming community. The senior member of the firm is Major T. J. Brown, who has been mentioned in connection with early history of Winston, and is a native of Davie County, N. C. Mr. Rogers is from Charleston, S. C. They have been associated together since 1878, and have a large trade throughout the surrounding country.

S. E. HOUGH, *Photographer*,

is a native of New York, was in the West Indies three years, and in New York twelve years. He is a fine artist, and his pictures give entire satisfaction. His rooms are large and conveniently situated on Main Street, Winston, and he enjoys a large patronage from the people and from the young ladies of Salem Female Academy. He keeps a large number of views constantly on hand of buildings and places of interest in the Twin-Cities.

W. A. WHITAKER, *Tobacconist, Winston*,

is a native of Yadkin County, and has had a wide experience in handling tobacco. His factory, on the corner of Church and Fifth streets, was originally built for a leaf house, is 44x116, having five floors, and with recent additions, is thoroughly equipped throughout. He employs about 150 hands, and has a capacity of fully half million pounds annually.

Mr. Whitaker uses only the leaf grown in the Piedmont section of this State. He is an expert buyer, and in his famous "Lucille" claims to have a product that cannot be excelled. White Wings, Coronet, Zip, Golden Slipper, Twin-City, Empress, Dick Graves, Peach and Honey, Olive Branch, and Ottar of Roses are among the favorite brands of this establishment. Mr. Whitaker is a progressive citizen as well as tobacconist, and has done much for the school system of Winston-Salem. The elegant electric light system which Winston has, its magnificent club-room, and various other public enterprises are largely indebted to his fostering care.

C. H. & C. A. Fogle,

under the firm name of Fogle Brothers, do an extensive business as Builders and Contractors. They are natives of Salem. Their great-grandfather was amongst the early settlers of Bethabara, and subsequently the family removed to Salem. Their father, Mr. Augustus Fogle, was Sheriff of Forsyth County many years, and afterwards Mayor of Salem. They have been engaged in the manufacture of Sash, Doors, &c., since 1871. Additional buildings and machinery were added from year to year as their business required, and the present two-story brick of plain architecture was erected in 1883. It is 60x120, filled with the best of plain and fancy sawing, planing and carving machinery, a fine equipment equal to any other in the State. The Arista Mills and many of the best business houses and private residences in the Twin-Cities have been built by them. Their dealings with customers are very liberal, and a large number of laborers and mechanics have secured homes by having long time payments that could not have done so otherwise. They turn out all kinds of building material, requiring about two hundred car loads of lumber annually, in addition to that purchased at the the saw mills in this section. Besides building material, they manufacture fifty to sixty thousand tobacco boxes annually, giving employment in different departments to seventy-eight workmen, making this a business of no small importance to Salem. They also keep employed in their comfortable office a lady stenographer and book-keeper.

The Wachovia National Bank of Winston

was established June, 1879. Mr. W. A. Lemly, the President, has been in the banking business many years, as he was elected Cashier of the First National Bank of Salem when only nineteen years of age, and occupied that position thirteen years, until the same stockholders established the Wachovia National, moved to Winston and elected him President. Mr. Lemly is a native of the county. Mr. James A. Gray, Cashier, was born in Randolph County, but came to Winston in childhood, and has been with the Wachovia Bank since the corporation was formed. Mr. Gray is owner of the handsome block of buildings which bears his name, a cut of which is shown in SOUVENIR. The bank regularly declares eight per cent. dividends, is popular with the people, and holds average deposits of a quarter million dollars.

## P. H. HANES & CO., WINSTON,

have the largest most extensive works for the manufacture of tobacco in North Carolina employing regularly five hundred skilled workmen. The firm consists of P. H. Hanes and J. W. Hanes, brothers, who were raised in Davie county, N. C. The elder was a boy soldier in the Confederate Army, and returned home to find the slaves freed, everything lost and the prospect of beginning life from the foot of the ladder. Being raised on a farm they have practical knowledge of the tobacco interests in this section. They had done a small tobacco business at Mocksville, but after the venture in seeking to make Winston a tobacco market, they were induced to move to the place and begin the manufacture of tobacco immediately in 1873. Commencing on small capital they had the misfortune to lose their buildings and equipments by fire in 1877, but soon afterwards erected about half their present factory which was afterwards extended. It is at present a four-story brick structure fronting one hundred and twenty-five feet and extending back one hundred and fifty-five feet with wings. They have in addition to the works used exclusively for manufacturing tobacco, a large shop for making their tobacco boxes with machinery—making the whole establishment complete in every particular. They have elegant office rooms, employ ten foremen, two book-keepers, one lady stenographer and keep two travelling men on road continually. They have an extensive wholesale trade from Maine to Texas, doing a large business in the latter State, as they give special inducements to secure that patronage. They operate upon a capital of over half a million dollars and are solid in every respect. They are prominent members of the M. E. church, South, employ some of their capital in public improvements and, are substantial and enterprising citizens of whom any place might well be proud.

www.ingramcontent.com/pod-product-compliance
Lightning Source LLC
Chambersburg PA
CBHW021526270326
41930CB00008B/1110

* 9 7 8 3 3 3 7 2 5 3 9 7 4 *